ADVANCED

TECHNIQUES
IDEAS IN ACTION
DIANA HOARE

GEORGIA DEAVER

ADVANCED

Calligraphy

TECHNIQUES
IDEAS IN ACTION
DIANA HOARE

NEW
BURLINGTON
BOOKS

A QUARTO BOOK

Published by New Burlington Books
6 Blundell Street
London N7 9BH
Reprinted 1995

ISBN 1 85348 161 0

This book was designed and produced by
Quarto Publishing plc
The Old Brewery, 6 Blundell Street
London N7 9BH

Senior Editor: Sally MacEachern
Art Editor: Andy Turnbull

Editor: Leslie Levene
Illustrator: David Kemp

Photographers: Ian Howes and Paul Forrester

Art Director: Moira Clinch
Editorial Director: Jeremy Harwood

Manufactured in Hong Kong by Regent Publishing Services Ltd
Printed by Leefung-Asco Printers Ltd, China

CONTENTS

INTRODUCTION

Georgia Deaver

THE CRAFT OF CALLIGRAPHY - a Greek word meaning beautiful writing - has roots which stretch back into the mists of time. The techniques, tools, materials and some of the letter forms are much the same now as they were in the Middle Ages, and further back, but this does not mean that calligraphy has no part to play in the modern world.

The Chambers Twentieth Century Dictionary defines "technique" as a "method of performance". This book is concerned both with working methods for practising calligraphers and with what they want their calligraphy to "perform" as a result of these "methods". In the West, we expect to see lettering running from left to right and from top to bottom in straight lines of varying lengths. However, the calligrapher has wonderful opportunities to break free from *the traditional mould and make letters perform visually as well as intellectually.*

The modern student of calligraphy turns to historical models for an understanding of letter forms as they were used by earlier professionals. Before the invention of printing, calligraphy was vitally important as one of the few means of storing and transmitting the written word. For centuries scribes produced books by hand and we have much to learn from their methods of working and their lettering skills.

Print is primarily for reading, not for seeing. The vast amounts of written material to which we are exposed every day make us switch off our sensitivity to lettering. Newspapers filled with sensationalism, information on every packaged product, road signs, shop signs and street names all bombard us. The act of reading has become an everyday skill that most of us take for granted.

Calligraphy helps us to "see" what we are reading by making the words beautiful. Much of its impact relies upon producing a rhythmic texture in the writing. This beauty, however, is not necessarily peaceful. Tensions can also be used to disturb us. Seen in this light, calligraphy is a powerful tool for communicating the written word in the modern world.

DIANA HOARE

RHYTHMIC TEXTURE

WRITING of any sort, whatever the style, creates a texture on the page by the rhythmic linking together of repeated shapes and patterns, and this texture of the lettering is one of its most important qualities.

To draw a comparison, knitting is given texture by the constant repetition of stitches, and different areas of texture can be made to contrast with each other. But just as a dropped stitch can ruin the texture of knitting, so a misshapen or badly formed letter can ruin the texture of a piece of lettering. Whichever alphabet is used, the creation of texture through the constant repetition of shape, form and movement is the basis of the calligrapher's art.

Traditionally, each part of every letter of all alphabets is related to the shape of the letter "O" of that alphabet. In this way a series of related strokes can be built up to form the complete alphabet.

It was the cider country more especially which met the woodland district some way off. The air was blue as sapphire such a blue that outside the apple region is never seen. Under the blue the orchards were in a blaze of pink bloom, some of the richly flowering trees running almost to where they drove along. Hardy.

Formal Italic
The formal italic "O" is an oval-shaped letter, slightly slanting. From this basis the rest of the alphabet is built up (above, right and below).

Foundational or Roundhand
In the Foundational hand (above top), the shape of the letter "O" is round. It is possible to write any letter of the alphabet over the letter "O" (above). Even the serifs are rounded, and a tiny round "O" can fit into them (below).

Gothic
The gothic adaptation of formal italic is based upon a sharply pointed, oval-shaped "O". The compressed nature of this hand makes a dark texture (above and right).

ʔOABOHNS

ON EITHER SIDE THE RIVER
LIE LONG FIELDS OF BARLEY
AND OF RYE THAT CLOTHE
THE WOLDE AND MEET THE
SKY AND THROUGH THE FIELD
THE ROAD RUNS BY TO MANY
TOWERED CAMELOT·AND UP
AND DOWN THE PEOPLE GO
GAZING WHERE THE LILIES
BLOW ROUND AN ISLAND THERE
BELOW THE ISLAND OFSHALOTT

Uncials
*Uncials are wide letter
forms based upon a round
"O". The letters create an
open texture, even though
they are written with little
space between the writing
lines (above and left).*

Versals
*The same is true of drawn
and painted capital
letters. Each letter of this
condensed versal alphabet
bears some relation to the
"O" shape in its
proportions. By drawing
the letter "O" you can
establish the proportions of
any other letter in the
versal alphabet (left and
below).*

ALL THE
WORLDS
ASTAGEG
ALL THE

OA OD ND

REQVI VE

By establishing a norm for the letters with a rhythmic texture the calligrapher can start to play with the size, position and colour of letters to create different moods and visual effects (right).

Here the spacing between the writing lines is varied. Also, spacing between the letters has been changed (right).

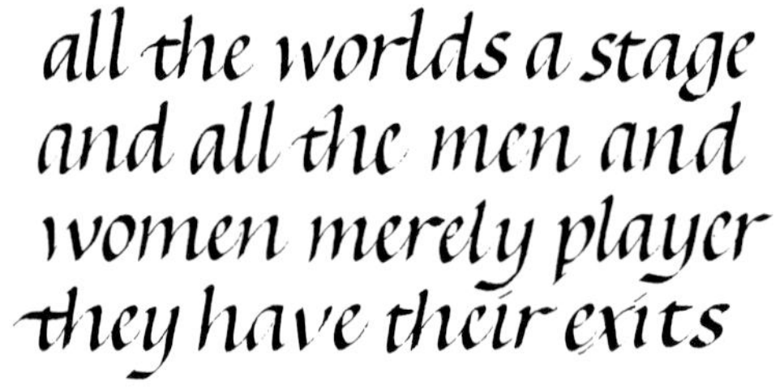

all the worlds a stage
and all the men and
women merely player
they have their exits

all the worlds a stage
and all the men and
women merely player
they have their exits

DIES IRAE DIES ILLA DIES IRAE
SOLVET SAECLVM IN FAVILLA
TESTE DAVID CVM SYBILLA
QUANTUS TREMOR EST FUTVRVS
QUANDO JUDEX EST VENTVRVS
CVNCTA STRICTE DISCVSSVRVS

The close texture in black and red creates an agitated mood (above).

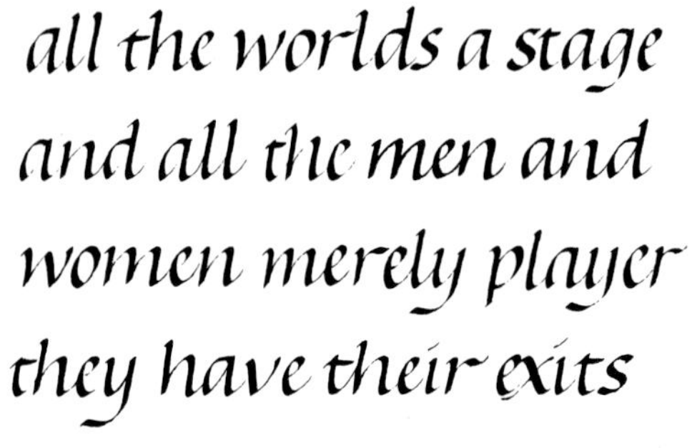

H·O·S·A·N·N·A I·N

E·X·C·E·L·S·I·S

The open texture in black and red creates a joyful mood (above).

EM MASS
RDI

Moving the angle of the letters from the vertical and the lines from the horizontal to form a circle gives a sense of peace (right).

REX TREMENDAE MAJESTATIS

The colour expresses a sense of majesty (above).

The regular ripples of the lines express the mood of the poetry (right).

Full Fathom Five Thy Father Lies;

Of his bones are coral made,
Those are pearls that were his eyes
Nothing of him that doth fade
But doth suffer a sea change
Into something rich & strange
Sea nymphs hourly ring his knell
Ding Dong
Hark how I hear them
Ding Dong Bell.

Letter styles are interwoven to depict the subtle harmonization of different voices in choral music (below).

The height of the letters has been increased and decreased for emphasis, while a letter is made to symbolize the cross (right).

KYRIE ELEISON CHRISTE ELEISON KYRIE ELEISON

SANCTUS

SANCTUS

SANCTUS

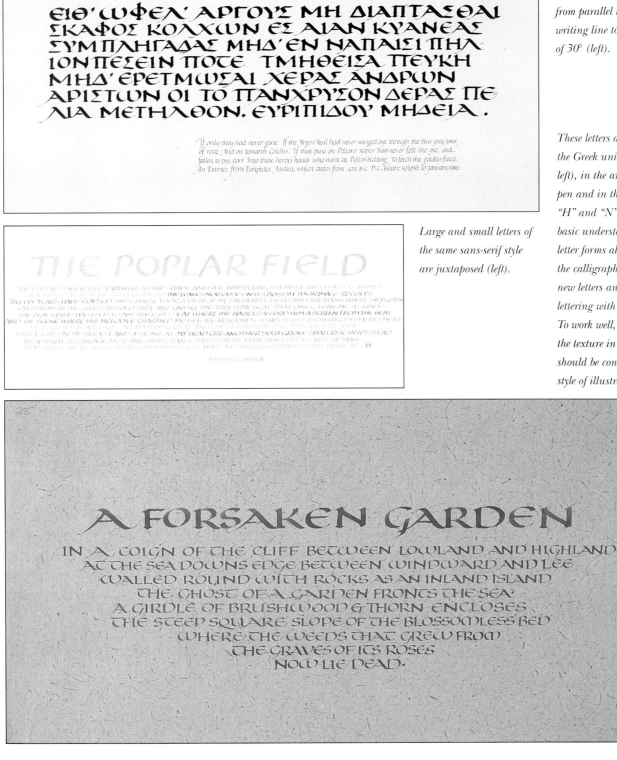

ΕΙΘ᾽ ΩΦΕΛ᾽ ΑΡΓΟΥΣ ΜΗ ΔΙΑΠΤΑΣΘΑΙ
ΣΚΑΦΟΣ ΚΟΛΧΩΝ ΕΣ ΑΙΑΝ ΚΥΑΝΕΑΣ
ΣΥΜΠΛΗΓΑΔΑΣ ΜΗΔ᾽ΕΝ ΝΑΠΑΙΣΙ ΠΗΛ
ΙΟΝ ΠΕΣΕΙΝ ΠΟΤΕ ΤΜΗΘΕΙΣΑ ΠΕΥΚΗ
ΜΗΔ᾽ ΕΡΕΤΜΩΣΑΙ ΧΕΡΑΣ ΑΝΔΡΩΝ
ΑΡΙΣΤΩΝ ΟΙ ΤΟ ΠΑΝΧΡΥΣΟΝ ΔΕΡΑΣ ΠΕ
ΛΙΑ ΜΕΤΗΛΘΟΝ. ΕΥΡΙΠΙΔΟΥ ΜΗΔΕΙΑ .

If only they had never gone. If the Argo's hull had never winged out through the blue grey jaws
of rock And on towards Colchis. If that pine on Pelions slopes Had never felt the axe, and
fallen to put oars Into those heroes hands who went at Pelias bidding, To fetch the golden fleece.
An Extract from Euripides Medea, which dates from 431 B.C. D.C. Hoare scripsit 10 January 1980.

These letters are similar to historic examples, but they have been adapted by changing the pen angle from parallel to the writing line to an angle of 30° (left).

THE POPLAR FIELD

Large and small letters of the same sans-serif style are juxtaposed (left).

These letters are more like the Greek unicals (above left), in the angle of the pen and in the forms of "H" and "N" (below). A basic understanding of letter forms also enables the calligrapher to design new letters and to combine lettering with illustration. To work well, something of the texture in the lettering should be conveyed by the style of illustration.

A FORSAKEN GARDEN
IN A COIGN OF THE CLIFF BETWEEN LOWLAND AND HIGHLAND
AT THE SEA DOWNS EDGE BETWEEN WINDWARD AND LEE
WALLED ROUND WITH ROCKS AS AN INLAND ISLAND
THE GHOST OF A GARDEN FRONTS THE SEA·
A GIRDLE OF BRUSHWOOD & THORN ENCLOSES
THE STEEP SQUARE SLOPE OF THE BLOSSOMLESS BED
· WHERE THE WEEDS THAT GREW FROM
THE GRAVES OF ITS ROSES
NOW LIE DEAD·

DECORATIVE POSTER

THE poster was to have two roles: it was to act both as a plan that would be useful for visitors to Michelham Priory and as an attractive souvenir. It therefore had to marry contrasting elements of formality and informality.

Formal and informal

The heraldry was executed in a modern style. This was colourful and formal at the same time. Heraldry contains both symmetrical and asymmetrical elements, and these played an important part in the design of the poster.

Italic was chosen for the text because it combines a degree of stylistic freedom with relative formality. The nib size was governed by the amount of information required. By using a small nib, compressing the writing and making the writing lines fairly close together, a dense black texture was obtained. This was lightened and given sparkle by the larger red titles, which relieved the heavy texture of the lettering, catching the eye and leading it on from paragraph to paragraph.

Drawing for the plan

Wherever possible decorative features of the map were used to provide opportunities for making pen-pattern textures. These helped to strengthen the relationship between the map and the text. The angle at which the pen was held was maintained so that the thick and thin qualities of the strokes would be constant and relate directly to the strokes of the lettering.

The tree symbol was made with a pen and then filled in. A strong pen characteristic was maintained throughout, and despite the "infilling", it was not a painted or drawn form but a pen-made shape. The process was reminiscent of the making of a versal letter. The outer shape was drawn with the pen at a 30° angle and the inner shape was then flooded

BRIEF:

To design a poster combining heraldry, text, map, illustrations and title.

TIME LIMIT: Two months.

SOURCES: Postcards, photographs, plans, guidebooks and transparencies.

DIMENSIONS: 60 x 46cm (24 x 181/2 in). The size had to suit the printer's laser-scanning equipment, since the map was to be used twice, once framed and hung in the entrance of the Priory, a second time as artwork for printing posters.

Formal symbols for the map: (right) ripples in the moat, (far right) freely flowing water; trees – first draw the outline, then flood in with a brush (bottom).

Experiments with free and formal italic meant that this free style version was discarded in favour of a formal version.

Plan of Michelham Priory

The intricate detail of Persian miniatures provided the inspiration for the style of illustration chosen.

with paint from a brush up to the pen outline. The arrangement of the tree symbols allowed for more decoration. Rather than being scattered at random over the area, they were arranged in a diaper pattern. This formal and stylized use of the pattern element tied in well with the stylized formality of the lettering.

Two different water symbols were used. They relied on the thick and thin qualities of the pen stroke, one suggesting the ripples in the water of the moat, the other indicating the freely flowing river water.

Illustration

The illustrations themselves were taken from the source material provided - postcards, guidebooks and photographs. I have evolved a style of illustration from studying Persian manuscripts, where there is a strong sense of pattern and decoration in the images.

Line drawings were made from the source photographs. The areas of different colours needed for different parts of the buildings were shown in this study but not fully completed. To make them more two-dimensional, they were presented head-on even if the original source showed the building at an angle. The outline of the buildings made an irregular shape on the page. The flat, two-dimensional qualities of these images complemented the two-dimensional qualities of the lettering, and the texture of the lettering was carried over into the texture of the pattern in the illustrations, in the detail of stone, brick and tile and of leaves, plants and flowers.

Title

The title was the linch-pin of the design as a whole. Various lettering styles were compared to see the effect of a contrast with the italic of the text, but the flamboyant colour and distinctive pattern of the heraldry placed at the top was providing sufficient contrast already. As a result, the italic style, with a large nib size, was finally chosen to unite all the lettering. The blue colour of the title made a link with both the heraldry and the map while providing a contrast with the black ink of the main text.

Design

Edward Johnston suggests that the ideal proportions for the margins of a broadsheet should be: 1:1.5: 2, and traditional, tried and tested solutions tend to work well. This format is based on the theory that the optical

A PLAN OF MICHELHAM
A PLAN OF MICHELHAM

Further experiments with lettering (top) Sans serif (bottom) uncial confirmed the choice of italic for the title - this would unite all the lettering.

centre of an object is higher than the actual centre - a rule that is important in the design itself. Thumbnail sketches help you to visualize how all the various elements will work together.

Since the information was fairly compressed, the text was broken up by illustrations and was written in narrow columns to make it more interesting and easier to read. The juxtaposition of text blocks and illustrations allowed for variety and movement within the formal composition. The weight of the pictures supported the weight of the text. The play of text against illustration created an asymmetrical balance. By contrast, the two balancing columns of text made an overall symmetrical design, with the plan forming the centrepiece. The two pictures of the Gateway Tower are echoed by the two columns, which themselves look like towers.

The 13 different heraldic shields which had to be incorporated into the poster were placed above the text with the title. This was to give the top of the page weight with which to balance the weight of the writing beneath.

Pasteup rough

Having decided upon the basic layout of the piece in a small pencil sketch, the next stage was to transfer this up to the size of the finished artwork. Working on a piece of layout paper of the correct dimensions, which in this case were 60 x 46 cm (24 x 181/2in), the size of the margins must be determined and ruled in pencil. You can then work on fitting the text and illustrations into the available space.

Lettering trials

Carry out lettering trials for the title and the text on separate pieces of layout paper with various nib sizes and spaces between the lines.

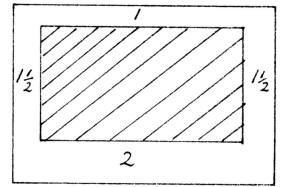

Using a photograph of the Priory as reference, a pencil drawing was made. The next step was a partial colour study exploring the textures of brick, tiles and windows (above).

Traditional margin proportions for a broadsheet (above).

The formal italic style chosen for the title (below)

A Plan of Michelham Priory

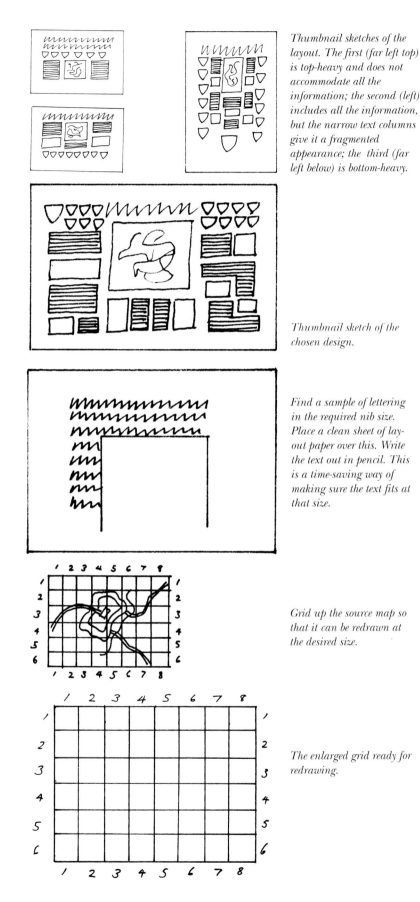

Thumbnail sketches of the layout. The first (far left top) is top-heavy and does not accommodate all the information; the second (left) includes all the information, but the narrow text columns give it a fragmented appearance; the third (far left below) is bottom-heavy.

Thumbnail sketch of the chosen design.

Find a sample of lettering in the required nib size. Place a clean sheet of layout paper over this. Write the text out in pencil. This is a time-saving way of making sure the text fits at that size.

Grid up the source map so that it can be redrawn at the desired size.

The enlarged grid ready for redrawing.

To establish if the text will fit into a given space in a certain nib size, write it out roughly in pencil instead of ruling-up, to save time. Working on a light table, place a piece of clean layout paper over a sample of lettering of the required nib size to act as a guide. If the text is too long, a smaller nib size or different spacing may be necessary.

A pen-written rough is the only way to establish with complete accuracy the line length and overall text block. This can then be cut up and pasted on to the rough.

Gridding up the map

The plan was adapted from a guidebook and redrawn to the appropriate scale by gridding up the source map and drawing another grid to the same proportions for the finished artwork. Having established the size and details of the plan in pencil, the decorative pen features were carried out in study form. This study was to establish exact colours and sizes of symbols, and was still an unfinished rough.

Once the study of the plan, the illustrations, heading, heraldry and text roughs had been completed on individual pieces of paper, they could then be assembled together on to a full-size rough. The final layout was considered and a pasteup rough was made.

All the loose pieces were put on to a sheet of layout paper over which a piece of glass was placed. This was done to prevent any distraction from the curled edges of the separate pieces of paper. Once the layout and positioning of the individual elements are satisfactory, they can be pasted up carefully so that all the edges are stuck down.

Artwork

The finished artwork must be very accurately ruled up and the illustrations and plan traced on before any work with ink or paint is begun. One way to achieve this is to rule the work up with a T-square on a drawing board with a straight edge.

The tracing of the illustrations, heraldry and plan can be made from the finished rough by using a light table. Place the finished rough pasteup on the writing surface of the light table and lay the paper for the finished rough, or even the final artwork, face up on top of the rough. The paper has already been ruled up at this stage, so you know exactly where the tracings are to fit. With the light table on, the images of the finished rough will be visible, even through heavy watercolour paper. In this way you can effectively redraw the image from the rough to the finished piece, without leaving any unsightly indentations from pressing too hard through tracing paper. Such marks are hard to conceal, even under paint.

Once the artwork is fully represented in pencil outline and the text ruled up, then work on the finished artwork can begin. Chinese stick ink, rubbed down with distilled water, and vermilion watercolour were used for the lettering of the text and the red titles. The illustrations and other coloured lettering were executed with artist-quality watercolour.

Beginning with the main title - possibly the most daunting part - the red titles were put in, and then the black writing, the painting of the heraldry and finally the illustrations.

The buildings were painted in flat blocks of colour and the details of brick, tile and stone were added when the flat colour was completely dry.

Text and calligraphy by Diana Hoare

The finished artwork ready for printing - 60 x 47.5cm (24 x 181/2in).

20

Michelham Priory

Map labels: Mallard · Anniversary Bridge · Heron · Moat · Kitchen Garden · Orchard · Dovecote · Shop · Canons Stew Pond · Main Entrance 1601 Century · CHURCH · Cloister · Well · (Site of church) · Stalle Footbridge · Augustinian Priory Founded in 1229 · Ancient Oak Trees · Restaurants · Site of Medieval Hall 14th Cent · Mallard · Canada Goose · Picnic & Playground Area

The Monastic Layout

The centre around which the buildings were grouped was the cloister, an expanse of turf some 70 feet square surrounded by a covered, paved walk. On the north side of the square stood the church running east west. The north walk is sheltered from the wind & sun although open & was used by the canons for teaching. On the east side stood the chapter house with dormitory above.

Existing Monastic Buildings

Of all the buildings so far described nothing remains above ground at Michelham; but the outlines of the church & western range have been revealed by excavation & marked on the ground. On the south side of the cloister stands the shell of the Refectory or Dining Hall although much altered since Tudor times.

The Watermill

was probably established in the 13th Century but the first recorded mention is dated 1434. It stands on a medieval site & has been rebuilt several times. The present oak framing dates from the 15th and 16th centuries with 18th century brickwork and nineteenth century weatherboarding. An iron waterwheel was installed in 1896 & was removed with other grinding equipment in 1925, when it ceased functioning as a working mill. The mill was restored to working condition in 1970 & now grinds local wheat into bread flour. The mill is powered by fall of water from the moat to the level of the river below. Diana C. Hoare scripsit April 1986. 27, Longburton, Sherborne, Dorset, DT9 5PG. Tel. Holnest 624.

...y Tower

...ior Leem about 1395 ...riginal condition. ...with Eastbourne green ...ing chalk & flint, ...et thick. The tower ...gh to the parapet & ...vide leaded walk ar... ...giving extensive ...ither side of the ent-

rance there were originally porters rooms. Two upper rooms have original floor timbers, interesting window sills & two, two-light windows. The present approach bridge is older than the tower and replaces an earlier drawbridge.

ILLUSTRATION

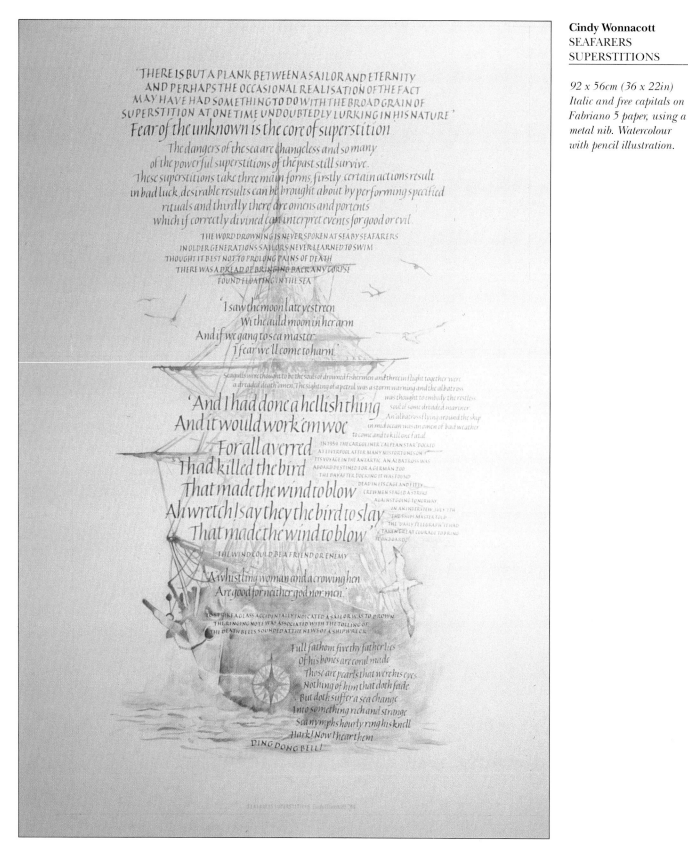

Cindy Wonnacott
SEAFARERS
SUPERSTITIONS

92 x 56cm (36 x 22in)
Italic and free capitals on
Fabriano 5 paper, using a
metal nib. Watercolour
with pencil illustration.

Denis Brown
POEMS FROM THE
CHILDREN OF LIR

54.5 x 41.5cm
(21 x 16in)
Initial page of manuscript
book. Gouache on
Edmunds Blue handmade
paper.

Denis Brown
EARLY IRISH
CHRISTIAN POEM

51 x 52cm
(20 x 20 1/2in)
Written in gouache on
Indian handmade paper,
with gold leaf on gesso and
gum bases.

ILLUSTRATING A BOOK

THE first task in a job of this size is to devise a cataloguing system capable of handling the sheer volume of references and information. Each of the 47 maps had to contain eight references - a piece of heraldry, two churches, two châteaux, a landscape, a grape type and a vine training method - making a daunting total of nearly 400 pictures.

Accuracy in every detail was paramount. I had to become an expert on the wine-growing areas of the world. In many cases information about these areas had to be taken from one map and combined with cartographic details of another. The spelling of all the names was painstakingly checked and rechecked. The colour of the illustrations had to match the source photographs. For the maps themselves, an accurate colour coding of the roads, rivers, boundaries, towns and wine areas was obviously essential.

I drew up a form showing where each reference was to be found. An envelope attached to each form proved invaluable for keeping cuttings and loose photocopies relevant to each map.

Adapting the references

The second stage involved adapting the pictures from the source material to the correct scale for use on the map. There was not enough time to redraw each of the pictures, so simplified tracings were made of the buildings, landscapes and vine training methods

BRIEF:

To illustrate a wine guide with 47 decorative maps, each to combine heraldry, architectural references, grape types, landscapes, vine training methods and a map.

TIME LIMIT: Three months, to include picture research and artwork.

SOURCES: Books on wine, architecture and travel, magazines and postcards.

DIMENSIONS: 30 x 45cm (12 x 18in), to be reduced to book dimensions of 157 x 197mm (6 x 8in).

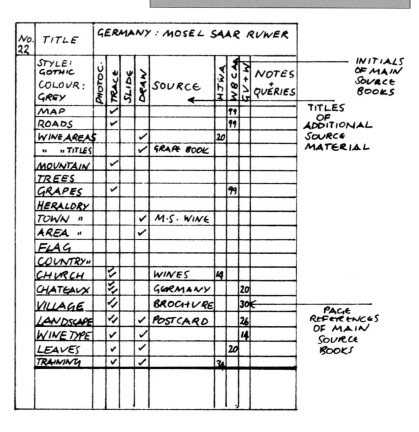

The finished artwork for Burgandy (far right).

A specifically-designed form was essential for keeping track of all the reference material and sources (right).

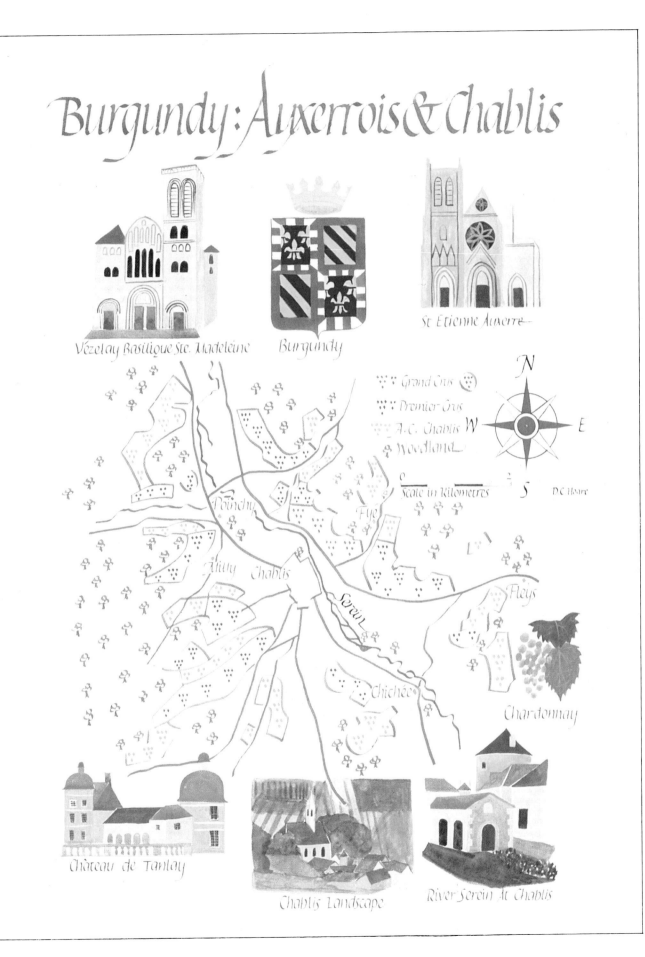

Burgundy: Auxerrois & Chablis

Vézelay Basilique Ste. Madeleine

Burgundy

St Étienne Auxerre

Grand Crus
Premier Crus
A.C. Chablis
Woodland

Scale in Kilometres

D.C Hoare

Poinchy

Fyé

Milly   Chablis

Serein

Fleys

Chichée

Chardonnay

Château de Tanlay

Chablis Landscape

River Serein At Chablis

directly from the sources. Since the scale of these tracings was often not suitable for the map, the tracings were enlarged or reduced by photocopier in batches. They could then be used at the appropriate size for the map in the finished paste-up rough.

The cartographic details of the maps and the wine areas were redrawn in colour from their sources so as to contain only the essential information about roads, rivers, boundaries, towns and wine areas.

The titles were designed so as to use a different style of lettering for maps of different areas of the world: France had italic; Germany, gothic; Italy, Roman roundhand; Eastern Europe, uncials. This helped to define the sections while maintaining the same feel throughout the book. For the roughs the titles were written out in their actual size and in colour on layout paper, ready for centring in the paste-up.

Paste-up roughs

The references were arranged on a sheet of layout paper by eye so that the composition was balanced in weight and the space was filled evenly. The format was portrait, with traditional margins of head 1: sides 1.5: tail 2.

When all the parts had been pasted in place, the sheet was photocopied. Many corrections had been done in the course of checking the information on the maps, so it was easier to trace through a new, single sheet of paper rather than through the paste-up.

Artwork

With work for reproduction, it is important to use white paper rather than cream so that the colour of the artwork is retained. The artwork here was done by request on an off-white paper, and then reproduced with a white background on white paper. As a result some of the tones of the original paintings were washed out along with the cream tone of the original background. If a cream background is required, it is better to use a cream paper for the book itself. The paper chosen was Heritage, a heavy, acid-free cartridge which did not cockle with the watercolour.

This commission provided a wonderful opportunity to make the most of rich colour in the titles, pictures, heraldry and the maps themselves. White pigment was mixed with the colours to make them bright.

Simplified line drawings were adapted from the reference photographs (above left).

The line drawings were the basis for the finished landscapes (above right).

The architectural references were traced in a simplified form (right).

The tracings were adjusted to fit each map by photocopying and enlarging or reducing (right).

Maps were redrawn in colour with all the relevant cartographic detail (right).

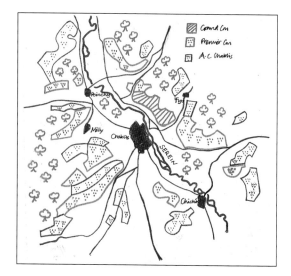

Italy: Piedmont

*Roundhand based on
Roman lettering was
chosen for Italy;*

GREECE AND CYPRUS

*uncials adapted from
Greek Uncial for Eastern
European maps;*

The Mosel Saar Ruwer Germany

*an adaptation of gothic
style for Germanic maps;*

Burgundy: Auxerrois & Chablis

*and a formal italic style in
reddish brown for France.*

*Paste-up rough in colour.
The small pieces of paper
were flattened under a
sheet of glass - this makes
them less distracting to the
eye when assessing the
design. The paste up was
photocopied for tracing up
the finished artwork.*

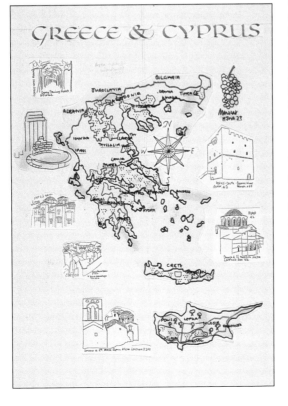

Transfer paper

A piece of tracing paper covered on one side with black lead pencil was used to trace the master copy on to the finished artwork. It is important to clean off surplus graphite from the tracing paper with a cloth. Pressing too hard while tracing leaves marks that are almost impossible to erase and are not always hidden by paint. The tracing paper was held on to the work by masking tape above the top margin of the map.

Tracing

All the lettering of the maps was traced on to the paper. Using a T-square, a line was also ruled for all of these. The title was ruled up and centred on the page and the captions were ruled up and centred under the pictures. After the lettering, the details of the map were traced on, making sure that no lines crossed the lettering, and then the pictures and heraldry.

The same order was used for the colour work. The colour for each word and each line had to be checked against the colours of the paste-up. All the main titles were completed together. The more lettering that can be done at the same time, the greater the consistency and flow of the writing. The lettering on the map involved using different pens for each colour simultaneously. Working from the top left-hand corner across and down the page helps to avoid smudging and to maintain the flow. This method was also used for all the roads, rivers and boundaries.

Texture

The texture of the map relies upon the use of a broad-edged pen to execute the decorative symbols. These can be used to the full to create pattern qualities. Throughout this series of maps the grape and the tree symbols featured prominently as decorative pattern-making textures.

Having completed the map, the illustrations were painted. Wherever possible, the colour was checked against the original photograph with the help of the reference form. Blocks of colour were applied first in artist-quality watercolour. The details of stone, tile and brick were added when the first paint was dry, with a very fine brush. The landscapes were painted last with flat washes of colour to tie them in with the flat style of the architectural references.

The 47 maps were prepared as finished artwork ready for photographing and printing in the book.

Text and calligraphy by Diana Hoare

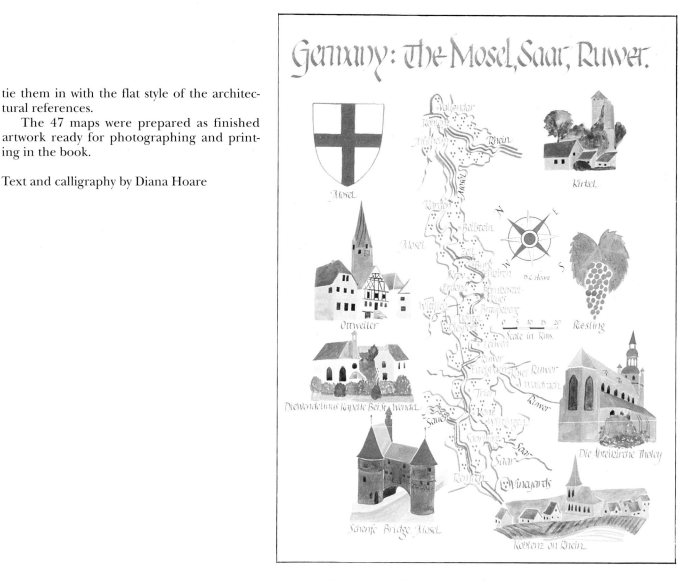

The finished artwork for the Mosel near Ruwer (above), Greece and Cyprus (right), and Italy, Piedmont (far right), ready for the printers– 30 x 45cm (12 x 18in). (By kind permission of Peter Dominic)

Italy: Trentino Alto Adige

Toblino Castle & Lake

Malvasia Del Chianti

Pinot Grigio

Meranese
di Collina
Merano

Valle Isarco

Terlano

Isarco

Caldaro

Bolzano

Santa
Maddalena

Colli
di Bolzano

Castel Corvia

N

W E

S

D.C. Hoare

Teroldego
Rotaliano

Valdadige

Sorni

Trento

Trentino

Casteller

Lake Garda   Adige

Wine Types
Towns

0   20

Scale in Km.

Telvana Castle

Trentino Landscape

Vines

29

AN ADVERTISING POSTER

THE client had suggested that a ruled white border all around the map would be a good way to display the area of paper without printing on it. However, when the map was drawn to scale, there was an area of white left around the land mass. I felt that this was very interesting in itself and that there was no need to force the map into a stark ruled border.

I decided to allow the parts of France which had no wine areas to bleed off the map, breaking through the white border in places and providing an interesting contrast to the areas of white.

Having established the dimensions of the map itself and its white border, work could begin on the landscapes and architectural references. Although the architecture was taken from photographic sources, the landscape was totally imaginary and pieced together around the main features.

BRIEF:

To produce a full-colour poster of a map of France showing wine-growing areas to promote a brand of paper. The wine areas and towns were to be labelled in calligraphy. The map was to be a collage of landscapes and architectural and pictorial references, bottles, grapes and market scenes. A large white border had to be incorporated into the design to show off the quality of the unprinted paper.

TIME LIMIT: Three weeks from start to finish.

SOURCES: Client provided books, magazines and other pictures.

DIMENSIONS: 60 x 90cm (24in x 35in)

Pencil sketch

The rough sketch of the map was begun in pencil. Line drawings of the architectural references were drawn in some detail, but the landscapes were only roughly sketched in

Thumbnail sketches to determine the position of the white border around the map.

The map was designed in detail in pencil and pasted up into a pencil rough. The landscapes are just sketched in at this stage (far right).

A small portion of the map was worked up into a colour study to explore ways of blending the architectural and landscape elements, as well as determining the colours (right).

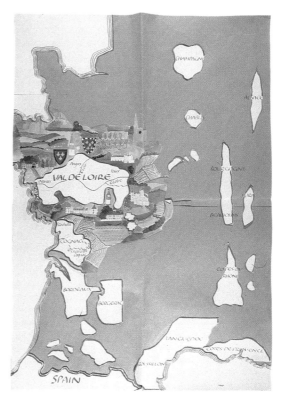

around these. Each pencil study was completed on a separate piece of paper and these were then assembled to make a complete pencil rough.

Colour study

The very tight time schedule did not allow for a complete colour study of the entire map. However, a limited colour study of a small area was carried out to explore the way in which the landscapes blended into one another and fitted around the architecture. In order to evaluate the relative weights of the blank wine areas and the heavier landscape background, the limited colour study was pasted up on to dark-green paper. This was to

approximate the colour value and density of the landscape background. White paper was pasted up in position to indicate the wine areas and the white border. This gave a fairly good impression of how the map would look when finished.

Artwork

The finished artwork was then traced from the pencil rough using transfer paper and the lettering was ruled up and written out. The detail of the landscapes was painted in as I went along.

Text and calligraphy by Diana Hoare

The white borders of the finished piece show off the quality of the paper advertised (right). (By kind permission of Pollock and Searby Ltd.)

The sea is indicated with a pen line which preserves the thick and thin qualities of the stroke, thus linking with the calligraphy of the wine area labels (below).

FAMILY TREE

THE size of the family tree was governed by the width of the wall on which it was to hang. The first stage was to plan the size of the lettering. Working on a very small section I lettered out two entries in what I thought would be an appropriate size. From this I was able to calculate whether the entire tree would fit into the available space.

Three nib sizes were used: a Mitchell no. 2 metal roundhand nib with black ink, a no. 4 with black ink and a no. 4 with vermilion watercolour. This last was for the note about partners of the bank.

The lettering was carried out in separate strips, generation by generation. These were then pasted up on to a larger piece of paper with the same amount of space between the generations.

Having established the approximate dimensions of the tree itself, I could decide where to put the title and crest. Owing to the pyramid shape of the tree and the fact that the founding member was to be given some prominence, I did not feel that a banner heading across the top of the composition was suitable. Instead, I decided on a column of lettering in the centre with the crest on one side, balanced by the title, golden bottle and address on the other.

The size and weight of the crest acted as a strong counterbalance to the amount of text in the right-hand bottom corner of the tree. The crest itself was drawn from a small embossed design on the cover of a book. The small drawing was enlarged as a pencil sketch to the required size. The rough was assembled on several pieces of layout paper held together with masking tape.

Artwork

Very heavy watercolour paper supplied in a roll was used for this project. In order to work on such a large scale it was necessary to enlarge my drawing board to accommodate the work. The drawing board was 0.9 x 1.2m (3 x 4ft), with a device for ruling parallel lines and a counterweight to help in adjusting the angle of the board. To this I screwed a 1.5 x 1.2m (5 x 4ft) piece of chipboard. A shelf was made to hold the roll of paper so that I could reach the top of the sheet.

The parallel ruling facility was invaluable for preparing such a large piece of ruling-up. Once the lines were ruled, the information from the finished rough was transferred in

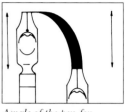

Amgle of the pen for writing versals.

To design a large family tree for a banking firm, showing partners and agents in the bank and a large heraldic crest. The design was to include a title and emblem in raised gold.

TIME LIMIT: Six months.

SOURCES: A typed copy, already set out as a family tree, was provided. With a project of this kind, it is essential to have clear, correct copy to work from.

DIMENSIONS: 1.5 x 1.2m (5 x 4ft)

pencil to the final artwork. In this way the information was accurately recorded before work began, thus significantly reducing the chance of mistakes creeping in later on.

Work began by completing the red versal letters of the title. These were executed in vermilion watercolour, with the drawing board at a fairly flat angle to allow the paint to flood into the letter outline without imme-

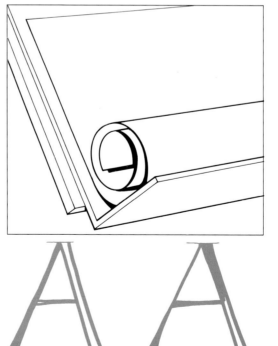

Shelf added to the end of the drawing board to hold the heavy roll of watercolour paper.

The outline of the versal letters is drawn with a pen and then flooded in with a brush.

diately pooling at the base of the strokes. The paint for these letters needs to be of a creamy consistency, thin enough to run through the pen easily, but thick enough to have a good covering quality and to give an opaque appearance to the finished letter.

The letter is constructed with a broad-edged pen held with the nib parallel to the writing line. The two outside strokes are drawn in place and the centre is then flooded in with paint from a brush. The letters themselves are based upon the Roman capital letters on Trajan's Column.

Work then began on the individual text entries. The lettering was carried out entry by entry, each one being completed before the next was started.

Corrections

The client wished to alter the information on one entry after this had been completed so a system of making corrections was devised. A small piece of sticky tape was placed over the letter which needed correcting. This was then gently rubbed down with an agate burnisher. Working very carefully but firmly, the tape was snatched upwards so that the ink surface of the letter and a little of the underlying paper was brought up with the tape. If any of the ink was left on the paper surface, the process was repeated. The paper was then prepared for writing by lightly burnishing down any loose fibres through a piece of rough paper with the agate burnisher. A dusting of very finely ground gum sanderac can be useful in reconstituting the paper surface and prevents it from bleeding on contact with the ink. The sanderac should be dusted off with a feather in firm strokes.

Painting

The painting of the crest was executed after the lettering had been finished. This was carried out with the board lying more or less flat. When the lettering and painting were completed the lines of descent were drawn in pencil with the ruling device. Then they were ruled in vermilion with a ruling pen and a short perspex ruler. It is very important when using a ruling pen to use the ruler upside down, to prevent the watercolour from running in underneath the edge.

Text and calligraphy by Diana Hoare

FAMILY TREE

The finished piece was framed and hung (right). (By kind permission of Messrs C. Hoare and Co.).

When using a ruling pen it is instinctive to use the ruler right side up. However, watercolour will seep under the ruler (left top). Always use a perspex ruler upside down. This ensures a neat line with no seepage (left below).

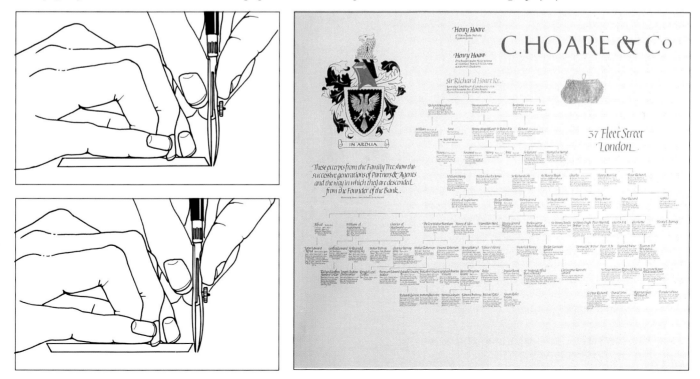

RAISED GILDING

THE final part of the work was the gilding. This was done on a raised gesso ground. The gold sticks to the gesso and is burnished to make it shine. For the gesso you will need: 16 parts slaked plaster; 6 parts white lead; 2 parts centrifugal sugar; 1-1.5 parts glue. The less glue that you can manage to gild with, the brighter the burnish will be, although it is harder to get the gold to stick to the gesso. It is essential to measure very accurately. One good way to do this is to put all the ingredients out separately in little spoonfuls on a sheet of paper so as not to lose count of how many spoonfuls you have taken.

Lay the gesso in outline with a nib. A flexible quill is ideal for this (top).

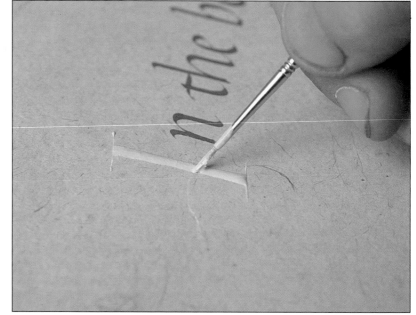

Flood the outline with a brush, so that one area is completely filled with gesso before it is teased on to the next. Make sure you pick up enough gesso to complete the flooding in one go (centre).

The gesso should be slightly raised; very high gesso is vulnerable to damage. Do not apply a second coat as different rates of drying will cause cracking. If there is a blemish on the wet gesso, fill with extra gesso; a bump can always be gently scraped away.

The ingredients should be mixed together and ground on a glass slab with a glass muller. The length of time for which they should be ground varies, but at least half an hour is probably necessary to ensure that everything is thoroughly mixed. It is best to grind without adding extra water. However, the mixture may be very stiff and if so, a few drops of distilled water may be added. When the mixture is thoroughly ground, it is turned out on to silicone-release paper in little cakes. When the cakes are dry, they can be peeled off and wrapped in tissue paper.

To prepare the dry cakes of gesso for use

Scrape gently with a sharp knife until the surface is smooth. The glue tends to rise to the surface when the gesso drys, making it hard for the gold to stick (top).

Rub gently with fine wet and dry paper (centre).

Finally, burnish the gesso with an agate burnisher. The smoother the gesso, the shinier the gold will eventually become (bottom).

they must be covered with distilled water. First, place the cake into a well such as those on a china palette. Then, cover it with water. Agitate it slightly with a small stick and leave it to soak. Continue the process, adding two or three drops of water at a time and stirring gently. You can also add two drops of thinnish gum ammoniac (see below) at this stage. This will enable you to gild successfully in any atmospheric conditions. When the gesso is more or less thin enough to lay, add three more drops of water and leave them sitting on

To lay the gold you need: a blowing tube of cartridge or stiffish paper fixed with tape; a gilder's cushion; a very sharp knife with 10cm (4in) blade; a Psilomelanite or agate burnisher with a point and flat surface, crystal parchment; a sharp, hard pencil; a book of loose-leaf gold (top).

Lay a sheet of gold directly from the book on to the gilder's cushion. Cut the gold generously, so that the gesso shape is well covered (centre).

Cut the gold firmly, pressing hard on the cushion, into squares of the required size (bottom).

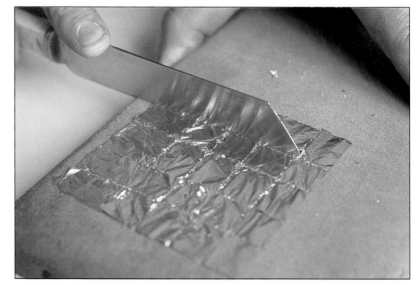

Blow on to the gesso through the tube to moisten it. If you have added gum ammoniac you will not need to blow so hard. Four long breaths should be enough.

the surface of the gesso. Any air bubbles that have got into the mixture will rise to the surface through the water and can then be burst. A few minutes later this is ready for use and you can start laying the gesso.

Flat gilding

The gold lettering in this piece was carried out using gum ammoniac. This can be prepared from the crystal form by soaking the gum crystals in water. After straining, the liq-

Pick up the gold on your forefinger before you start blowing. Rubbing your nose to pick up some grease first will help it stick. As soon as the gesso is damp, lay the gold over the shape and press down hard with tissue. Rub down with your finger.

Push the gold into the edges of the gesso with a sharp pencil. Work the tip of the burnisher around the shape, pressing the gold into the edges. Burnish the gold through the crystal parchment. Next burnish the surface directly.

uid must then be gently heated in a saucepan and strained again several times before it is ready to use. It must be thin enough to run through a pen.

As for versals, the drawing board should be at a fairly flat angle for using gum ammoniac in a pen. This prevents the gum from pooling in the base of the letters. When it is dry, the letters can be breathed on gently and the gold laid on to them. For this kind of gilding, it is sometimes easier to use transfer leaf than loose-leaf gold. Transfer leaf is actually attached to sheets of paper in a book and can be very useful when gilding complicated shapes or lines of writing.

Pressing down hard with the flat surface of the burnisher, polish until the gold shines brightly. Use the pointed tip to burnish around the edges. This ensures the gold sticks firmly all around as well as polishing it.

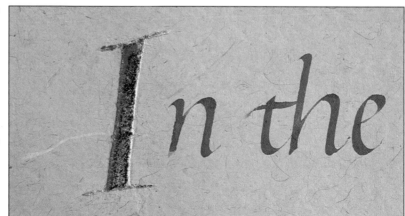

If you need a second layer, lay it on the burnished surface without breathing on it. If there is a hole which needs repairing, remove all loose bits of gold before breathing on it. Lay the second sheet on the first. Press down with tissue paper. Burnish first through crystal parchment then directly.

To decorate a plain gold surface with dots or lines draw the pattern on to crystal parchment and trace through it directly on to the gold with a hard pencil.

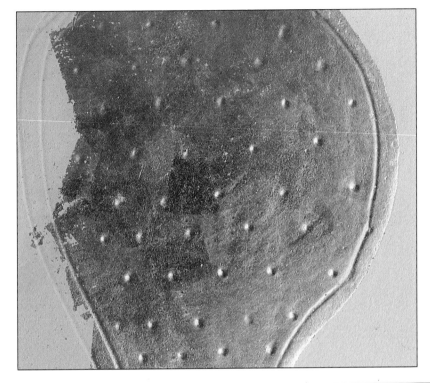

Be careful not to pierce the crystal parchment with the pencil and scratch the gold. However, you must press hard enough to indent the surface of the gold and the gesso beneath.

An example of gilded lettering, the outlines add emphasis to the letters.

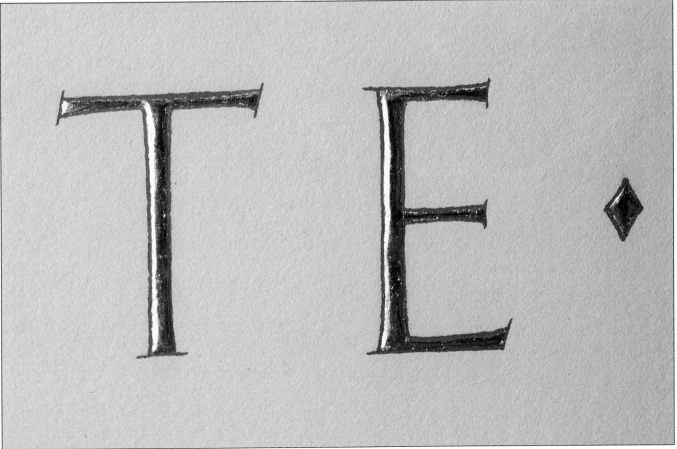

GILDING

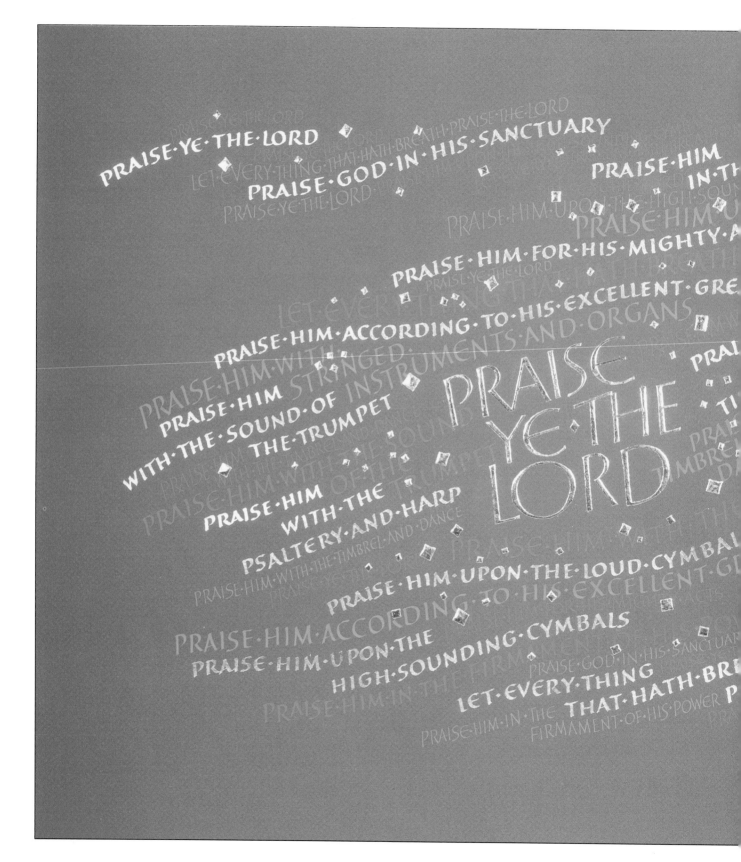

IRMAMENT OF·HIS·POWER
THE·LOUD·CYMBALS

HIM·PRAISE·YE·
TH·THE THE·LORD
REL·AND·DANCE
PRAISE·HIM·WITH
RINGED·INSTRUMENTS
AND·ORGANS

PRAISE·HIM·
FOR·HIS·MIGHTY·ACTS
SE·THE·LORD
PRAISE·YE·THE·LORD

THE ARMS OF
THE URBAN DISTRICT
COUNCIL OF
CLACTON

GRANTED 1936

LUX FELICITAS
SALUBRITAS

ARMS

Party per chevron,
azure and gules: the
upper part semé of
cross-crosslets and

David H. Nicholls
PRAISE YE THE LORD

100 x 72cm (39 x 28in)
Written out in raised and
burnished gold, transfer
gold and gouache, with
quills on BFK Rives
printmaking paper.

Denis Brown
DETAIL OF
HERALDIC PANEL
(CLACTON)

24 x 90cm (91/2 x 35in)
complete
Gouache and bronze
powder on Ingres paper
and a mount covered in
the same paper.

IN LOVELY HARMONY

THE WOOD HAS PUT ON ITS GREEN MANTLE,

& SUMMER IS ON ITS THRONE

PLAYING ITS STRING MUSIC,

HUSH! LISTEN! THE WORLD IS ALIVE

NINETEENTH CENTURY WELSH VERSE · THOMAS TELYNOG EVANS · ARTIST/SCRIBE · STAN KNIGHT 1985

THE SEASONS

THE main inspiration behind *The Seasons* was my interest in mosaics. The composition has a formal, external structure made by the circles and a formal, internal structure made by the mosaic of coloured lettering.

I had planned to make a manuscript book in which each section would be devoted to a season and contain poetry from a number of different sources. Each page would reveal a new image. The challenge of a broadsheet, however, is to direct the eye from one piece of poetry to another even though they are on the same page.

The visual effect of the poetry has not been expressed in the lettering, except for an imposed idea of colour - warm colours for the hotter months, cold colours for winter. Where it has been explored, as in the trailing pea blooms, this has been principally to assist the movement of the eye across the design rather than to present the image of a pea bloom or a landscape.

External structure

It is easier to begin with a black and white rough. *The Seasons* divides neatly into four parts. I superimposed this overall structure on the mosaic of lettering by placing the names of the seasons in a band at the top and bottom of the design. I chose versals because they

The versal letters are spaced in pencil.

Next the letters are drawn in pencil.

The letters are redrawn in colour, slightly widening the letters of spring.

Pasteup colour study for the lettering in watercolour.

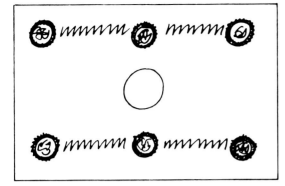

A thumbnail sketch determines the external structure of the design.

The circles are divided by a Yin Yang symbol of life.

Spots of gold link the sun with the planets.

The final representation of the sun was reached after trying out several different versions.

are lively and contrast with the rigidity of the design. Versals are a painted letter style, here executed in watercolour, which links them with the illustration of the astrological signs. Each of the names of the seasons has the same number of letters, but the letters in summer, autumn and winter are wider than those in spring, so they had to be compressed slightly. The bands of versal letters incorporated circles representing the signs of the zodiac, arranged around the central circle of the sun. These signs act as corner stones in a rectangular frame. The structure as a whole is an attempt to impose an intellectual view of the universe upon the words.

In order to include all 12 signs, I used the symbol for life based on the Chinese *Yin* and *Yang* to divide the circles. The style of illustration was taken from medieval bestiaries, in which animals are often contorted into curious shapes. Some of the designs have been made up from spots of colour to resemble the texture of a mosaic. The sans-serif capitals around them are also like pieces of mosaic.

To link the star signs and the sun together, the figures were painted and then decorated with little spots of gold: on the claws of the crab, the horns of the ram and the hooves of the bull, for instance. The use of gold in this way can be very effective. The flashing of the light off small areas can be far more exciting than a mirror-smooth slab of gold.

Internal structure

The formality of a mosaic is continued in the internal composition of the piece. Poems written in sans-serif capitals are arranged in narrow columns at either side to complete the rectangular effect. The strip of dense lettering running across the centre of the work is very important in the overall structure of the design. It acts both as a dividing and a linking element: the eye is encouraged to follow the line of lettering through the centre circle and over to the other side; it is also held by the stillness of the orange, centred lettering beneath the sun, where it is poised on the vertical axis like reflected light.

For each of the seasons I found a quotation which seemed to encapsulate in one sentence the spirit of that season. They make a loud statement that sticks in the mind and give each quarter a block of writing that is large enough to form a good texture.

The first version of the
sun was surrounded by
seasonal landscapes
(above).

The next stage was to convey a sense of the cyclical movement of the seasons. The zodiac moves through the sky as the year slowly passes. Visually this sense of movement was already emphasized through the division of each of the zodiac circles. The repetition of the Yin and Yang symbols of life gives a feeling of spinning movement to the rest of the page.

Roughs

I made several colour roughs for this piece. The eye is led around the design by the use of slowly changing colours. This echoes feelings of changing temperature and nature's progress throughout the year. The outside borders of the piece also reflect these colour changes. The colours of the versals and the zodiac symbols summarize the colours used in the rest of the lettering of that season, while in their weight and size, they contrast with it. The mosaic of words was given cyclical movement by extending the curved lines of "and now the sonne hath reared up his fyrie head". These letters are like flames shooting out of the sun. The lettering is attempting to illustrate the meaning of the text and at the same time give a feeling of movement to the composition as a whole. The rigid structure was

also relaxed by interweaving the lettering in the spring and summer panels and making them more energetic. "Tossing his mane" and "the juicy wheat" were given flourishes.

The sun

The symbol of the sun is the focal point of the composition. As the centre of the mosaic it is static. Contained within the stillness, however, there is considerable energy. Visually, the sun as the blazing centre of the universe is a potent image. And in the words used, the sun is seen as the centre and source of all spiritual life. The quotation gives the sun a Godlike,

A full colour paste up
entailed compositional
changes and provided an
opportunity to check all
the wording.

The second version of the sun was stylized, set against a textured background.

ic lettering around the central circle seemed far too bland for the meaning of the words.

The idea of the sun's rays bursting through the compressed versal letters seemed to work as an abstract representation of the words. The energy of the idea was reflected in the energy of the letter forms. The broken texture of the versals made them like pieces of mosaic.

The horizontal points of the sun were omitted as there was already a strong horizontal line across the centre. The emphasis on the vertical is also made with the rays. The energy of the sunburst is made by the gold lines, which break through the rings of capital letters and explode into the main body of the text.

Gilding

The gold in the central design was both raised and flat. The circle in the middle of the sun was raised gold and burnished quite highly. The large gold rays and the thin gold lines of the sunburst, and the gold features of the figures were all executed in flat gilding with gum ammoniac. (For the recipes and methods of preparation for raised and flat gilding see Family Tree).

all-seeing quality: "I am the eye with which the universe beholds itself and knows itself divine", from Shelley's "Hymn to Apollo". This is a good example of how effective lettering, used in conjunction with a symbol, can be when the poetry itself is so strong.

My first idea had been to combine the lettering with illustration and to place a stylized face in the centre of the gold on the sun. In four quarters round this I planned to portray a different landscape, one for each of the four seasons. This developed into a stylized sun set against a textured background of leaves and branches reflecting seasonal changes. Neither of these versions really worked. They were too realistic in their illustration and the use of ital-

The raised gesso for the sun was laid first. The outside shape of the large rays was painted in with a narrow brush using gum ammoniac, which was then flooded into the outline with a larger brush. The surface of the gum should be slightly raised. It should be flooded in very smoothly, with no dimples or uneven areas. The gilding of the zodiac figures was also done with gum ammoniac laid by brush. Although gum ammoniac may be lightly burnished after it is dry and before the gold is put down, this must be done through a piece of crystal parchment. If you were to use the burnisher directly on the gum itself, it might very easily be dented or damaged. Once the gold is laid on the gum, the heat made by the burnisher's rubbing on it might easily damage the gold surface. This problem with friction means that gold laid on gum ammoniac can never be burnished very highly.

The thin rays of the sunburst were ruled in gum ammoniac with a ruling pen. This should be done with a perspex ruler which is used upside down to prevent the gum from running in under the ruler.

The gilding of such narrow rays is best done with transfer not loose-leaf gold. You can make transfer gold from loose-leaf gold by rubbing a leaf of tissue paper with a candle. Enough candle wax is left on the tissue to make the gold stick to the paper.

Text and calligraphy by Diana Hoare

SEASONS
106 x 76cm (42 x 30in).
The composition is
inspired by mosaics.

GO SUMMER

AUTUMN

of yellow hue
ows with delight

ful as Spring

eels grow and trailing
pea blooms ope
their velvet eyes
and weeds and flowers
in their summer
liveries appear
for summers
liveries boast unnumbered
dyes.

y lush

soote

rtu
h inspired
he yonge

The juicy
wheat
now spindles
into ear

O thou who passest through our vallies in
Thy strength, curb thy fierce steeds allay the heat
That flames from their large nostrils Thou, O Summer
Oft pitchedst here thy golden tent and oft
Beneath our oaks hasslept while we beheld
With joy thy ruddy lips and flaming hair.

There lies a subtle lusciousness around
The far streched pomp of summer which the eye
Views with dazzled gaze and gladly bounds
Its prospect to some distant views that lie
Nesting among the hedge confining grounds
Where in some nooks the haystacks newly made
Scents the smooth level meadowland around
While underneath the woodlands hazely hedge
The crowding oxen make their swailey beds
& in the dry dyke thronged with rush & sedge
The restless sheep rush in to hide their heads.

When now no more the alternate
twins are
fired and cancer
reddens with the
with the
solar blaze
short is
the doubtful
empire
of the night.

AND NOW THE
SONNE HATH
REARED UP HIS FYRIE
FOOTED TEME MAKING
HIS WAY BETWEEN
THE CUPPE & GOLDEN
DIADEM. THE
RAMPANT LION
HUNTS HE FAST
WITH DOGGE OF
NOISOME
BRETH

IAM THE EYE WITH WHICH
THE UNIVERSE
BEHOLDS ITSELF &
KNOWS ITSELF DIVINE

low
st
ing,

and

THE TREES ARE UNDRESSING & FLING IN MANY PLACES ON THE GREY ROAD
THE ROOF THE WINDOW SILL THEIR RADIENT ROBES & RIBBONS & YELLOW LACES
A LEAF EACH SECOND SO IS FLUNG AT WILL HERE THERE ANOTHER & ANOTHER
STILL AND STILL A SPIDERS WEB HAS CAUGHT ONE WHILE DOWN COMING
THAT STAYS THERE DANGLING WHEN THE REST PASS ON.

Season of mist and mellow frutfulness
Close bosom frend of the maturing sun
Conspiring with him how to load and bless
With fruit the vines that round the thatch eaves run
To bend with apples the moss'd cottage trees
And fill all fruit with ripeness to the core

I SAW OLD
AUTUMN
IN THE
MISTY
MORN
STAND
SHADOW
LESS LIKE
SILENCE
LISTENING
TO SILENCE
FOR NO
LONELY
BIRD
WOULD
INTO HIS
HOLLOW
EAR FROM
WOODS
FOLORN
SHAKING
HIS LANGUID
LOCKS ALL
DEWY BRIGHT
WITH
GOSSAMER

raid
tine

That time of yeare
thou mayst in me behold
When yellow leaves or none
or few doe hange
Upon those boughs which
Shake against the cold
Bare ruined quires
where late the
swete bird
sang.

lved
rows or
ment.

O Wild West Wind thou breath
of autumns being.

Thou from whose unseen presence the leaves dead are driven like ghosts from
an enchanter fleeing Yellow & black & pale & hectic red Pestilence stricken multitudes
O thou who chariotest   to their dark wintry bed
the wingèd seeds.

A CALENDAR

A FEW months before beginning this piece I had been to the British Museum, London and made drawings of several artifacts, not knowing when or how I would use them. One object was an Anglo-Saxon brooch consisting of several smaller circles set around a central one. The design seemed eminently suitable as a basis for this particular project.

The text I chose was from Thomas Hardy, whose work includes pieces on woodlands and seasonal occupations such as cider-making and tree-planting. Having decided upon the design and the text, I began to work on a black and white sketch of the calligraphy. The next step was a pencil rough which established the exact position of each element. Seeing the design in black and white rather than colour helps you to look at it as an abstract pattern, and thus to decide whether all the various elements are working together.

The first colour rough was executed on cream-coloured paper. It is very important when using subtly graded watercolour to work on a white background, otherwise the colours tend to appear muddy.

The outer rim of the wheel was designed in red. The main colour of the piece was green and the eye cries out for the complementary colour of red to relieve it. The red band is broken with the little green zodiac signs, which relate it to the green centre of the composition.

The design at the centre of the piece was taken from a book of signs by Rudolph Koch and is thought to represent the eight points of the heavens. I thought that this emphasized the intention of the calendar while providing an interesting centrepiece to the design.

The finished piece was very carefully ruled up. When each line was in position, the lettering was pencilled in. This is the only way to ensure that no mistakes work their way into such large and complex pieces of work. The pencil should be used very lightly to prevent the lines from showing under the watercolour paint. When the lettering is complete and the paint is dry, the writing lines can be removed carefully with an eraser.

Basic design questions are best resolved in an initial, rough, black and white sketch.

The next step is a detailed pencil rough. The initial design has been modified; the large capitals in the centre unify the design (right).

A colour rough was only begun when every detail of the overall design had been decided (below).

Text and calligraphy by Diana Hoare

A TREE CALENDAR OF THE SEASONS & YEAR

A CALENDAR
76 x 76cm (30 x 30in)
The white paper makes the colours sparkle. Greens are light and yellow-based; darker, blue-greens tended to deaden the overall effect (above).

Detail showing how the leaves have been painted with thick watercolour to give an opaque effect. Adding a little white to the paint increases the opaqueness.

HEDGEROWS

THE possibilities for using calligraphy as a propaganda weapon or as a medium for conveying facts are very exciting. With this piece I was initially captivated by the startling fact that every year nearly 8,000km (5,000 miles) of hedgerow in Britain are lost through changes in farming practices. I began to work on ideas for a design in which such a dramatic statement about the destruction of the country landscape could feature prominently. I collected further information about the history of hedges, their function as a habitat for fauna and flora, and the methods of cutting and laying or pleaching hedges. I also used two John Clare poems and a passage from Thomas Hardy.

Lettering is about the creation of textures. For this piece I was inspired by the textures of the landscape outside my workshop window. There are sweeping views across fields and hedges to a distant range of hills. The different fields - corn, stubble, red ploughed earth, grass, root crops, hops - and orchards provide numerous different colours and textures, which change constantly as sunlight and cloud play across them.

Tree textures also played an important part in my mind: bare branches against a grey sky, trees in full summer foliage, autumn

Inspiration was drawn from the nature around me, such as the strong architectural shapes of tree trunks and branches silhouetted against the sky (right and below).

The texture of cut and laid hedges - a traditional method of managing hedges in England - inspired the texture of the words (left).

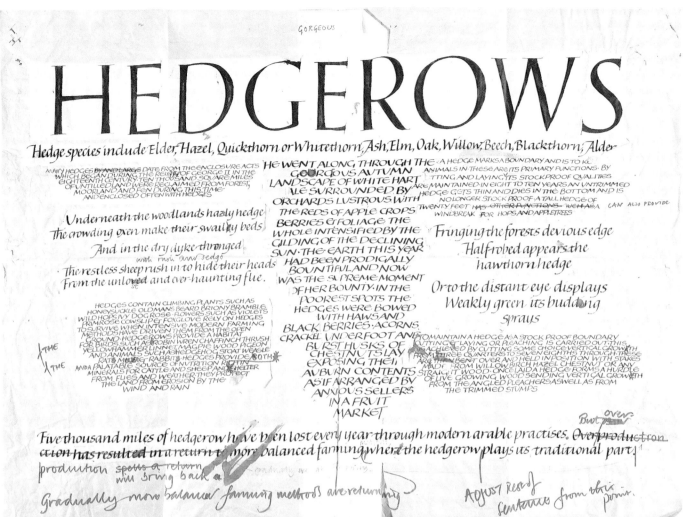

The paste up rough allowed for checking the wording and adjusting the design (above).

The texture and colour of bark and stones contributed to the overall effect of the finished piece (left and right).

leaves against a bright-blue sky, or the architectural strength of a tree trunk; even the texture of bark, fallen leaves on the grass, apple trees smothered with blossom or encrusted with golden and red fruit.

The arrangement of the lettering follows the lines of a fairly traditional layout, although there is variety and movement within the design itself. The title is echoed by the important quotation across the foot of the broadsheet, which gives it some prominence. The blocks of information about hedges have a tight, interlinking texture which is reminiscent of the interwoven branches of the cut and laid hedge. The lettering is executed in watercolour which blends and changes throughout, so that no two letters are the same colour. This gives a harmonious feel to the colouring of the piece.

Text and calligraphy by Diana Hoare

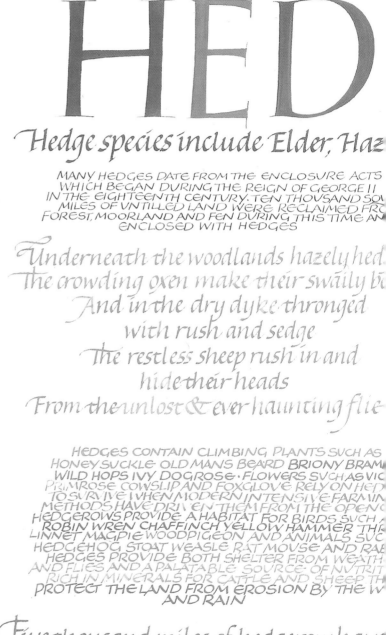

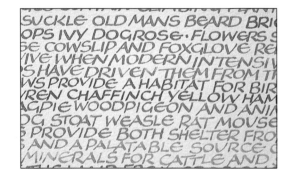

Lettering inspired by the texture of the cut and laid hedge (left).

GEROWS

uickthorn, Ash, Elm, Oak, Willow, Beech, Alder, Holly.

WENT ALONG THROUGH THE GORGEOUS AUTUMN LANDSCAPE OF WHITE HART VALE SURROUNDED BY ORCHARDS LUSTROUS WITH THE REDS OF APPLE CROPS BERRIES AND FOLIAGE THE WHOLE INTENSIFIED BY THE GILDING OF THE DECLINING SUN · THE EARTH THIS YEAR HAD BEEN PRODIGALLY BOUNTIFUL & NOW WAS THE SUPREME MOMENT OF HER BOUNTY · IN THE POOREST SPOTS HEDGES WERE BOWED WITH HAWS AND BLACKBERRIES ACORNS CRACKED UNDERFOOT & BURST HUSKS OF CHESTNUTS LAY EXPOSING THEIR AUBURN CONTENTS AS IF ARRANGED BY ANXIOUS SELLERS IN A FRUIT MARKET

A HEDGE MARKS A BOUNDARY AND IS TO KEEP ANIMALS IN · THESE ARE ITS PRIMARY FUNCTIONS · BY CUTTING AND LAYING ITS STOCKPROOF QUALITIES ARE MAINTAINED · IN EIGHT TO TEN YEARS AN UNTRIMMED HEDGE GETS THIN IN THE BOTTOM AND DIES AND IS NO LONGER STOCKPROOF · A TALL HEDGE OF TEN OR TWENTY FEET CAN ALSO PROVIDE A WINDBREAK FOR HOPS OR APPLES ·

Fringing the forests devious edge
Half robed appears the
hawthorn hedge
Or to the distant eye displays
Weakly green its budding
sprays.

TO MAINTAIN A HEDGE AS A STOCKPROOF BOUNDARY CUTTING AND LAYING IS CARRIED OUT · THIS IS ACHIEVED BY CUTTING SOME CHOICE VERTICAL GROWTH FROM THREE QUARTERS TO SEVEN EIGHTHS THROUGH · THESE ARE THEN BENT OVER AND HELD IN POSITION WITH STAKES MADE OF WILLOW BIRCH HAZEL CHESTNUT OR ANY STRAIGHT WOOD · ONCE LAID A HEDGE FORMS A HURDLE OF LIVE GROWING WOOD SENDING VERTICAL GROWTH FROM THE ANGLED PLEACHERS AS WELL AS FROM THE TRIMMED STUMPS ·

n lost every year through modern arable practises but gradually rning where hedgerows play their traditional part. ⊞ scripsit.

HEDGEROWS
52 x 80cm
(201/2 x311/2in) The
arrangement of the lettering
is traditional, but the design
conveys the variety and
movement of the landscape.

OAK AND ASH

WHERE lettering is to be accompanied by illustrations, there obviously has to be a relationship between the lettering and the style of illustration. However the calligrapher can bring words to life by illustrating their meaning with lettering alone. This opens endless avenues for exploration.

Oak and Ash is an attempt to portray a wood through lettering. The piece was inspired by woods in Dorset, England. Instead of illustrating the poems which describe the wooded landscapes, I have used the colour and shape of the letters in the tree names to suggest trees, and also used colour and texture in the writing of the poetry to suggest some of the landscapes portrayed in the words.

First, looking into this imaginary wood, the eye can focus on the tree names as if they were trees in the foreground with the poetry as background. When seen as background to

Detail of tree names representing trees in the foreground (right).

Woodland scenes which inspired this piece of calligraphy.

The rough colour paste-up allowed for refinement of the design and checking that the words were correct (below).

Detail suggesting undergrowth, leaf canopy and woodland floor textures (left).

the trees, the poetry has many textures. It can resemble undergrowth, leaf canopy and the woodland floor. Alternatively, one can look past the tree names, deeper into the poetry, to explore a variety of different woodland landscapes. When seen this way, the lettering of the poetry portrays different landscapes, such as a group of pine trees, a pathway or distant wooded hills seen beyond the wood itself.

In the design, by placing the tree names and poems evenly around the broadsheet the reader's eye is allowed to wander freely. I am trying to express the feeling of walking at will through a wood. The viewer is led on from passage to passage to inquire further into the piece.

Rather than leave a white hole inside the letter O of Oak, a small, light-textured piece in italic was chosen to fill the gap. The overall quality of the letter form, which lies in its

Detail of poetry - the content of the words presents changing vistas and views to the imagination (below).

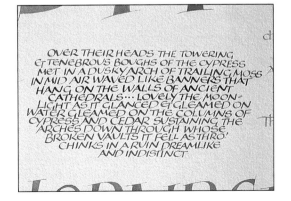

ASH

strength, size and beauty, is kept. The contrast of textures which characterizes the rest of the design is carried into the open texture of the letters.

Although the white space on the broadsheet is filled evenly, the eye is led first to the large letters of "Oak" and "Ash" which form the title. The style of the lettering of these words was designed to reflect something of the qualities of the trees themselves. The broad, ancient oaks are like the large, classically strong Roman letters which depict them. Originally, these Roman letters were designed and executed with a chisel-edged brush. However, once you understand how the letter forms originated, they can be drawn with a pencil and then painted, using different colours. The word "Ash" was the second element to be designed. This is a less substantial tree, one which always gives a sense of rushing movement when the wind blows through its leaves. These versal letters are based on the Roman letter forms, but they have been adapted to be written more freely. The shape of the letters is slightly reminiscent of ash twigs.

The use of colour in the piece is two-fold. Each of the larger letters has been painted in several shades of one colour, but within the blocks of lettering as a whole there is considerable movement of colour.

Text and calligraphy by Diana Hoare.

Versals give a sense of movement, reflecting some of the qualities of the ash tree (above).

OAK AND ASH
106 x 76cm (43 x 30in)
The colour and shape of the lettering combine with the texture of the design to convey the atmosphere of a wood (right).

The large Roman letters reflect the qualities of the oak tree (below).

OAK

WILLOW

ASPEN

THE LEAVES OVER HINTOCK UNROLLED THEIR CREASED TISSUES & THE WOODLANDS SEEMED TO CHANGE FROM AN OPEN FILIGREE TO A SOLID OPAQUE BODY

last rose as in a dance the stately trees & spread their branches hung with copious fruit their blossoms gemmed.

MY ASPENS DEAR WHOSE AIRY CAGES QUELLED QUELLED OR QUENCHED IN LEAVES THE LEAPING SUN

BEECH

The woods decay the woods decay and fall The vapours weep their burthen to the ground

SYCAMO

*Detail of poetry
representing background to
the trees (right).*

HAZEL

But see the fading many coloured woods Shade
deepening over shade and the country round im-
brown a crowding umbrage dusk and dun of every
hue from wan declining green to sooty dark.

TO THE
MAN
OF
IMAGIN·
ATION
NATURE
IS
IMAGIN·
ATION
ITSELF

WYCHELM

The roaring dell o'er wooded narrow deep
And only speckled by the midday sun
Where its slim trunk the ash from rock to rock
Flings arching like a bridge;
that branchless ash
Unsunned and damp whose few poor leaves
Ne'er tremble in the gale yet trembles still
Fanned by the waterfall.

How
Pleasant
NEATH THE
WILLOW BY
THE BROOK
THAT'S KEPT
ITS ANCIENT
PLACE FOR
MANY A
YEAR
TO SIT AND O'ER
THE CROWDED
FIELDS
TO LOOK & THE
SOFT DROPPING
OF THE SHOWER
TO HEAR
OURSELVES
SO SHELTERED

LARCH

As when upon a tranced summer night
Those green robed Senators of ancient woods
Tall oaks branch charmed by
ernest stars dream.

SILVER BIRCH

THE POPLARS
ARE FELLED
FAREWELL
TO THE SHADE
AND THE
WHISPERING
SOUND OF THE
COOL
COLONNADE

AK

THE
OAK
BEFORE
THE
ASH
WE'RE
SURE
TO
HAVE
A
SPLASH

I stood on Brockans sovran height and saw
woods over woods, hills over hills
A surging scene only limited
By the blue distance

AND
HERE
WERE
FORESTS
AS
ANCIENT
AS
THE
HILLS
EN
FOLD
ING
SUNNY
SPOTS
OF
GREENERY

THE
ASH
BEFORE
THE
OAK
WE'RE
SURE
TO
HAVE
A
SOAK

HAZEL

But see the fading many coloured woods Shade
deepening over shade and the country round im-
brown a crowding umbrage dusk and dun of every
hue from wan declining green to sooty dark.

ASH

Here waving
groves a
chequered scene
display
And part exclude
and part admit
the day
There interspersed
with lawns &
opening glades,

QUICKBEAM or ROWAN

OVER THEIR HEADS THE TOWERING
& TENEBROUS BOUGHS OF THE CYPRESS
MET IN A DUSKY ARCH OF TRAILING MOSS
IN MID AIR WAVED LIKE BANNERS THAT
HANG ON THE WALLS OF ANCIENT
CATHEDRALS··· LOVELY THE MOON-
LIGHT AS IT GLANCED & GLEAMED ON
WATER GLEAMED ON THE COLUMNS OF
CYPRESS AND CEDAR SUSTAINING THE
ARCHES DOWN THROUGH WHOSE
BROKEN VAULTS IT FELL AS THRO'
CHINKS IN A RUIN DREAMLIKE
AND INDISTINCT

WE PAUSED AMID THE PINES THAT STOOD
THE GIANTS OF THE WASTE
TORTURED BY STORMS TO SHAPES AS RUDE
WITH STEMS LIKE SERPENTS INTERLACED
A SPIRIT INTERFUSED AROUND A THINKING SILENT
LIFE TO MOMENTARY PEACE IT BOUND OUR MORTAL NATURES
STRIFE AND STILL IT SEEMED THE CENTRE OF THE MAGIC CIRCLE
THERE WAS ONE WHOSE BEING FILLED WITH LOVE THE
BREATHLESS ATMOSPHERE

HORNBEAM

WATERCOLOUR WASHES

MANY writing surfaces, including those which can be cut into like wood, glass and stone, have inspired the calligrapher. Finding a good-quality surface that will take ink and is not too rough or too smooth is a constant problem. Flecks of fibre in paper and pore marks and different colourings in vellum make good backrounds for calligraphy. In Anglo-Saxon times vellum was frequently stained purple to set off the lettering or gold. But vellum is expensive to buy and requires considerable skill and patience to prepare. However, in an exciting combination of calligraphy and painting, you can create your own backgrounds by using colour washes over the coarse surface of watercolour paper.

Good-quality watercolour papers are made by machine, mainly from cotton. They are evenly white and are a little too rough for writing very fine lines. Handmade papers are often tinted and some contain an interesting amount of fibre from flax, which is made into linen, or other papermaking plants. Most handmade papers have a pattern of "laid" lines, which come from the mesh or "deckle" on which they were made. Wove papers do not have these lines.

Most modern papers have size added to the pulp, rather than being sized later as completed sheets, or tub sized, as handmade papers traditionally used to be. To prevent the watercolour wash from affecting the sizing in the paper some modern watercolour papers are tub sized as well. Even so, in order to write over a layer of watercolour pigment, this new surface has to be sized by a dry method using ground sanderac to stop the ink from bleeding into the pigments.

Watercolour pigments

It is useful to understand something of the chemistry of watercolour pigments. Those mentioned in the list below divide into two groups: soluble stains and insoluble, sedimentary colours. By understanding this principle

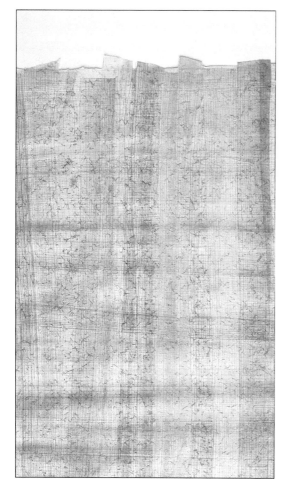

Papyrus, made from an aquatic plant, was used as a writing surface by the ancient Eyptians, Greeks and Romans (left).

Vellum for calligraphy is usually a calfskin which can be prepared as a writing surface (right).

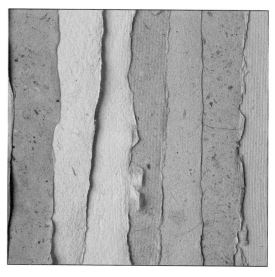

A selection of handmade papers of varying colours and textures, showing the deckle edge (right).

Make a second fold in the cover to allow for the thickness of the pages (left).

direction, running parallel with the chain lines. As with all books the paper is cut so that the grain direction is parallel with the spine.

When the pages are cut and folded, fit the book neatly inside the cover by knocking up the edges on the work bench. Mark a line between 6-10mm ($1/_4+3/_8$in) in from the spine and mark four holes along this line: one at the head and one at the tail (these should be the same distance from the edge as from the spine; the other two holes spaced evenly between them).

Use a pair of dividers to set the distance.

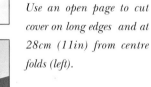

Use an open page to cut cover on long edges and at 28cm (11in) from centre folds (left).

Fold the cover in to the central folds (right).

Work the sewing in a figure of eight, tensioning the thread as you go. Finish by tying a reef knot (right).

The finished book (left).

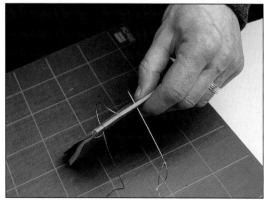

The stab-stitching restricts the book's opening. This must be taken into account when spacing the letters of the alphabet on the page (right).

Pierce the holes with a thin awl. Thread a needle with the mercerized cotton and knot the thread on to the needle.

Single-section binding

Combining the weak pages of a single section binding with a tough cover made from millboard and leather can be a problem. One possible solution is to use thread to act as the only hinge between the two. In this way one can avoid creating a tension between the pages and the cover when the book opens.

A strip of thin leather, reinforced by a strip of aerolinen is sewn on to the pages using a figure of eight stitch (right).

The cover opens out separately from the pages, which are held only by the thread (left).

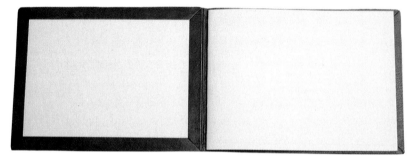

With the cover open flat the leather strip is pasted out with starch paste. It forms a 45° mitred joint with the leather turn-ins of the cover (above).

Multi-section binding

The purpose of a design binding is to attract the reader. The cover is a vehicle for the binder's self-expression. The binding itself needs to be protected in a box.

The problem of making the soft watercolour paper compatible with heavy boards and leather is solved by sewing each fold of paper on to a strong, flexible support, linen tapes, which are in turn attached to the boards. The linen tapes act as the hinges for the boards, rather than the leather. The leather has no part in the structure of the binding. The linen tapes also act as a flexible backbone for the pages so that they can open out flat.

The structure of the book

Text and bookbinding by William Taunton

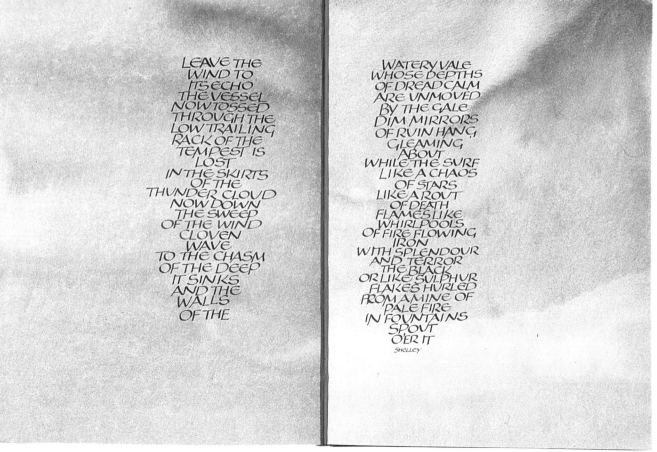

A VISION
OF THE
SEA

TIS THE TERROR
OF THE TEMPEST
THE RAGE OF
THE SAIL
ARE FLICKERING
IN RIBBONS
WITHIN THE
FIERCE GALE
FROM THE STARK
NIGHT OF VAPOURS
THE DIM RAIN IS
DRIVEN
AND WHEN
LIGHTENING IS
LOOSED LIKE
A DELUGE
FROM HEAVEN
SHE SEES THE
BLACK TRUNKS
OF THE
WATERSPOUTS
SPIN

AND BEND
AS IF
HEAVEN
WAS
RUINING IN
WHICH THEY
SEEMED TO
SUSTAIN WITH
THEIR TERRIBLE
MASS
AS IF OCEAN
HAD SUNK
FROM BENEATH
THEM: THEY PASS
TO THEIR
GRAVES
IN THE DEEP
WITH AN
EARTHQUAKE OF
SOUND AND
THE
WAVES
AND THE
THUNDERS
MADE
SILENT
AROUND

The calligraphy is written in dark blue watercolour on 300gsm (140Ib) watercolour paper over multi-coloured watercolour washes (left and below).

LEAVE THE
WIND TO
ITS ECHO
THE VESSEL
NOW TOSSED
THROUGH THE
LOW TRAILING
RACK OF THE
TEMPEST IS
LOST
IN THE SKIRTS
OF THE
THUNDER CLOUD
NOW DOWN
THE SWEEP
OF THE WIND
CLOVEN
WAVE
TO THE CHASM
OF THE DEEP
IT SINKS
AND THE
WALLS
OF THE

WATERY VALE
WHOSE DEPTHS
OF DREAD CALM
ARE UNMOVED
BY THE GALE
DIM MIRRORS
OF RUIN HANG
GLEAMING
ABOUT
WHILE THE SURF
LIKE A CHAOS
OF STARS
LIKE A ROUT
OF DEATH
FLAMES LIKE
WHIRLPOOLS
OF FIRE FLOWING
IRON
WITH SPLENDOUR
AND TERROR
THE BLACK
OR LIKE SULPHUR
FLAKES HURLED
FROM A MINE OF
PALE FIRE
IN FOUNTAINS
SPOUT
O'ER IT
SHELLEY

End papers were made from a fold of watercolour wash paper (right).

The cover is dark blue goatskin with coloured goatskin onlays that reflect the sea imagery of the poems (far right).

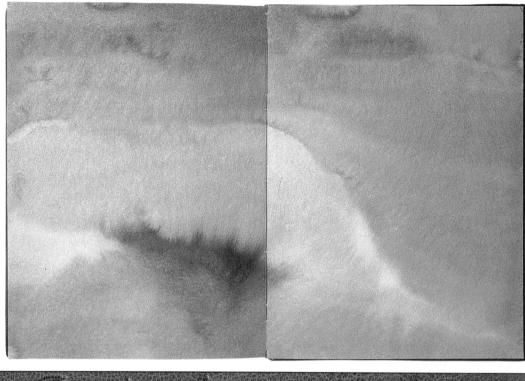

Tooled cover with onlays for single - section binding (below).

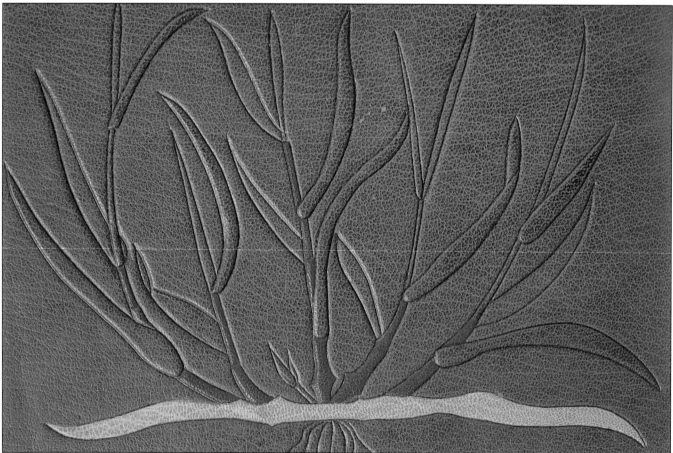

LETTERING IN CUT PAPER

THE calligrapher learns that the shape of the letter derives directly from the use of the square-cut pen. Cut paper involves the use of a different tool, a sharp pair of scissors or a craft knife, and the character of the letter form changes accordingly.

In this project, the letters are cut freely in paper, without any preliminary drawing. It can be useful to use newsprint, as the printed columns give a rough guide to the size of the letter being cut, and letters cut in thin black paper work well. The basic form is that of a traditional letter, but natural variations arising from the use of the new tool are exploited and allowed to develop. The family relationships of letters, learned from calligraphy, are respected, but the character of the letter reflects the direct cutting action of a pair of scissors or a craft knife. This can result in a somewhat angular letter form and the round letters present interesting problems. *Alpha and Omega* and *Home Sweet Home*, show some ways in which this problem has been resolved. Letters cut with a knife will be subtly different in form from those cut with scissors.

Method

Work on soft board and stab-pin the cut-out letters into position on their appropriate background. Adjustments are easily made by altering or discarding and recutting the letters. They can be changed and moved around until the right balance between letter shape and space is achieved and you feel the whole design presents a satisfying unity. This method enables you to keep a careful watch on the background spaces, those important areas inside and between letters, between words and

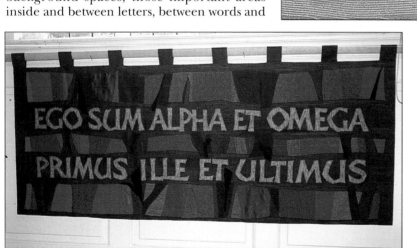

ALPHA AND OMEGA
Pat Russell and Elizabeth Ford 68.5 x 280cm (8 x 21/3ft)
Hanging in free appliqué and machine stitching, based on cut paper letters (left).

HOME SWEET HOME
Pat Russell 30 x 56cm (161/4 x 221/4in)
Cut paper lettering was used as a pattern for a panel in layered and cut net and machine stitching, mounted on fabric (above).

between lines. Considerable patience and much hard work is required at this stage, but it is worth persevering until you are happy with the design. You can then paste down the letters accurately in position.

Alternative forms

Another form of cut-paper letter can be built up from small strips of paper, each element of the letter being cut separately. This method is extremely flexible and can result in original, lively lettering. Since these letters are not pen-made, the distribution of their thick and thin strokes need not necessarily correspond to that of traditional letter forms; instead their placing is governed solely by the demands of the design. This works well with both capital and lower-case letters. *Home Sweet Home* was designed in this way, the elision of the letter forms developing spontaneously from the method of design used. Two fabric versions are shown, each based on the original cut-paper master pattern, one in layered and cut net, the other in coloured felts. In the second, the colour emphasis is on the spaces between the lettering, giving an entirely different aspect to the design.

Cut-paper lettering may also be used in graphic design and the paper collage can stand as an art form in its own right. The use of torn paper provides added dimension, the characteristic rough edges and uncertain outlines producing letters of a very different nature from the cut variety.

Text and lettering by Pat Russell

HOME SWEET HOME
Pat Russell 38 x 46cm
(15 x 18in)
Small banner in coloured felt. Colour emphasis is on spaces between the letters (above).

BEVERLEY
Student's work in progress using torn paper.
(Metchosin Summer School of Arts, Victoria, B.C.)
Letters can be changed and moved until correct balance is achieved (right).

CALLIGRAPHY ON CLOTH

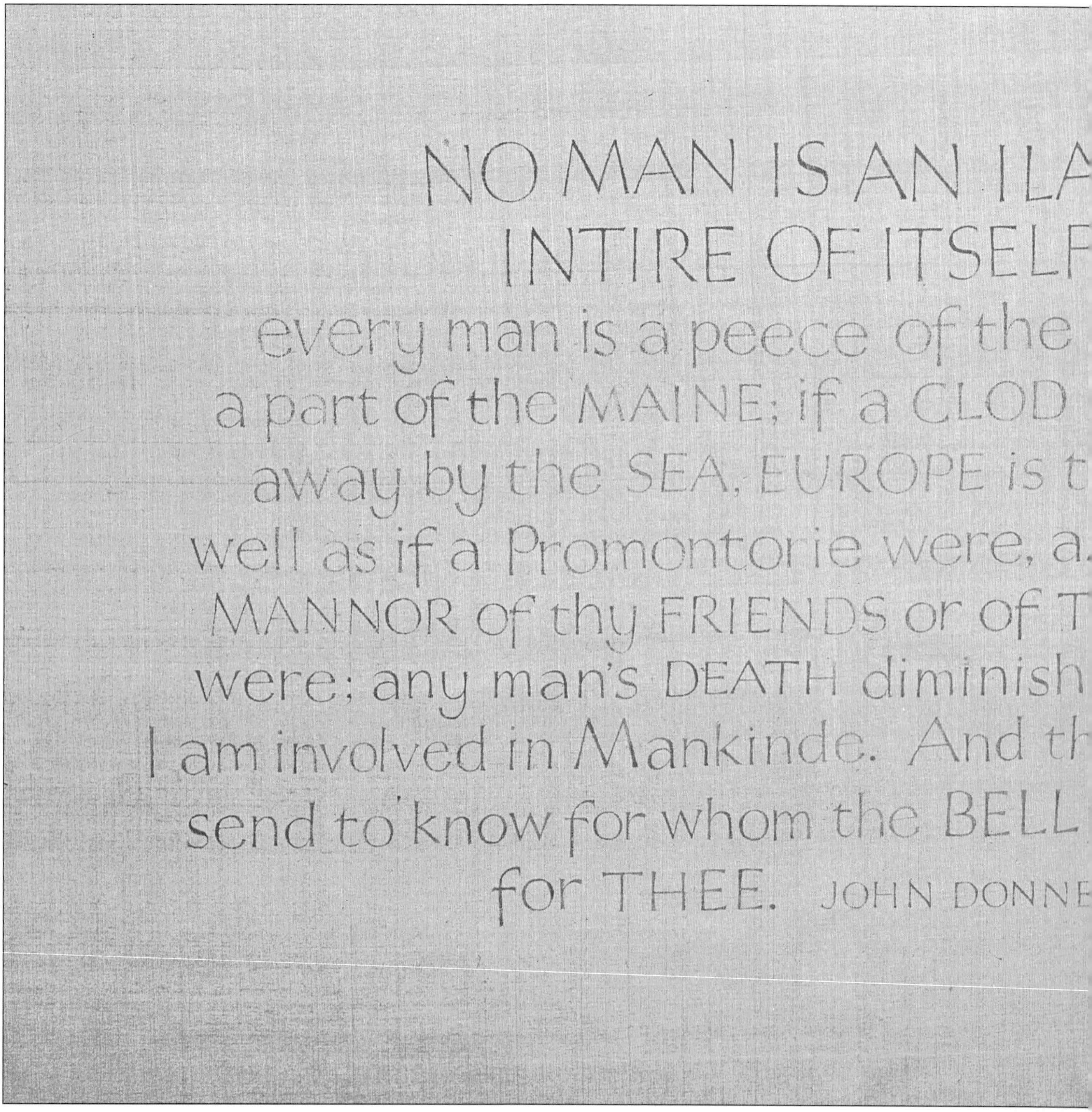

NO MAN IS AN ILA
INTIRE OF ITSELF
every man is a peece of the
a part of the MAINE; if a CLOD
away by the SEA, EUROPE is t
well as if a Promontorie were, a.
MANNOR of thy FRIENDS or of T
were; any man's DEATH diminish
I am involved in Mankinde. And th
send to know for whom the BELL
for THEE.   JOHN DONNE

Brenda Berman
NO MAN IS AN
ISLAND

61 x 46cm (24 x 18in)
Watercolour on Chinese
silk.

Denis Brown
ARIES

*20 x 13cm (8 x 5in)
Brush painted letters in
gouache and bronze powder
and raised and burnished
gold on gesso. Paper was
crumpled lightly while wet
and dyed. Where the paper
was creased more dye was
absorbed.*

D

NTINENT,

e washed

lesse, as

ell as if a

NE OWNE

ME, because

efore never

ls; it tolls

3—1631

Susan Hufton
WARM RAIN LADEN
EAST WIND

*120 x 87cm (47 x 34in)
Each panel 38 x 87cm (15
x 34in)
Detail from a triptych. The
background layer is of raw
silk with a leaf pattern
made by sponging gouache
around leaf-shaped
templates and then
embroidering the veins.
The remaining two layers
are of silk organza; the
watercolour letters have
been painted on the top
layer with a pointed brush.*

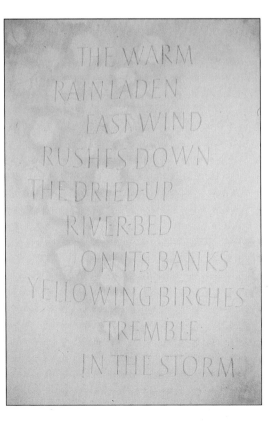

ALPHABET DESIGN

WHY bother to design new alphabets? Apart from the obvious benefits of experimenting free from any constraints, as a letter designer, my overriding interest has always been with the letter forms themselves and with an awareness that letters, as well as performing their function as "signs for sounds" can also be contemplated as pleasing in their own right. Alphabet designs stress this contemplative aspect and encourage the viewer's attention to turn towards the letter forms. The very familiarity of our alphabet means, unfortunately, that we seldom take the time to observe letters closely.

It is surprising how, even among some people who work with letters, the forms of letters are taken for granted as a fixed number of styles to be mastered: Roman, italic, uncial, and so on. It is as if letters are seen as something external to us, as shapes to be copied and not as forms which can be re-created in the imagination and therefore endlessly modified and adapted for different materials, processes and purposes. Through this internalizing operation, the art of letter making can be kept alive and perpetually renewed in the minds of each new generation. As A. K Coomaraswamy said, "it is of the essence of tradition that something is kept alive".

When working with the letters of the alphabet and considering the potential for varying the forms, I am constantly reminded of Herbert Read's remark on the abstract painting of Ben Nicholson: "The simplicity and fewness of the formal symbols employed by this artist do not constitute a limitation on his powers of invention - on the contrary he revels in the multiplicity of the variations he can command with these limited means".

Alphabet One

If you examine the first alphabet design, its most obvious element is the dynamic pattern which the letters make over the surface of the slate. The letters have affinities with classical inscription forms, both in their proportions and in having a stem width of about one-tenth of the letter height. With horizontal strokes about half the width of vertical stems and with the vestiges of calligraphic influence in, for instance, the shape of the bowls on "B", "P" and "R", the relationship with classical sources is further underlined. In other ways they clearly differ from traditional Roman letters, most

Having selected the most promising sketch, the alphabet was drawn on a larger scale of 28 x 11cm (11 x 41/2in) to clarify the idea and resolve design details (right).

The first step in designing Alphabet One was to make a series of rough 18 x 8cm (7 x 3in) sketches (bottom).

ALPHABET ONE
56 x 22cm (22 x 9in)
Incised on black slate,
painted off-white using
signwriters paint (left).

noticeably in the forms of "C", "G", "O", "Q", "S" and "U", the slope forwards and the lack of serifs, which gives the letters a more streamlined, pared-down quality.

Edward Johnston was concerned in his approach to his work and in his writings to give starting points (the Foundational hand being the obvious example) and to show that letter forms were "capable of great development".

The letters in Alphabet One can be seen as a development from Roman capitals. Comparing the "O" of a Roman letter with the "O" shape in this alphabet, you can see that while the former is more or less circular, the latter has a form which, though related to a circle, has a shape which has been slightly distorted, giving emphasis to the top part of the letter. It also has three thin points instead of the usual two. All this has the effect of making the form active within the rectangular format of the slate.

The "O", being the key for other curved forms, sets a pattern for curve formation throughout the design. "C "and "G" do not literally follow the shape of the "O" but preserve a relationship with it. "S has a close correspondence in structure with the "C" shape. Stems

ALPHABET TWO
38 x 38cm (15 x 15in)
Incised black slate

are weighted slightly towards the top to enhance the sense of growth and movement.

Alphabet Two

This is a compressed and somewhat squarish-looking alphabet, which can be seen as an intermediate stage between the letters in Alphabet One and the tall, narrow letters in Alphabet Three. The letter "R" has changed from a straight-tailed form to one with a more flowing tail, which fits in more uniformly with the other letters. The square shape of the slate reinforces the shape of the forms.

Alphabet Three

This design is a combination of the forms in Alphabet One and a related, narrowed and angularized form, taking the idea of compression a stage further to produce a striking and unusual form. The piece is an experiment with different sizes, weights and forms of letters but depends on the fact that though different, the letter forms have a definite link with one another.

Finally, I experimented with three letters - "A", "R" and "C" - taking forms similar to the tall, narrow forms in Alphabet Three. These are used as a basis from which to develop an abstract arrangement of diagonal and curved lines of varying thickness which cut right through the edges of the slate.

I have tried to show, however briefly, something of how one idea leads to another and to suggest other possibilities. Each person will need to establish their own reference points and grow into their own perspective.

Text and letter carving by Tom Perkins

ARC
61 x 15cm (24 x 6in)
Incised black slate, painted
off-white (left).

ALPHABET THREE
48 x 15cm (19 x 6in)
Incised black slate, painted
off-white (right).

VARIED EXAMPLES

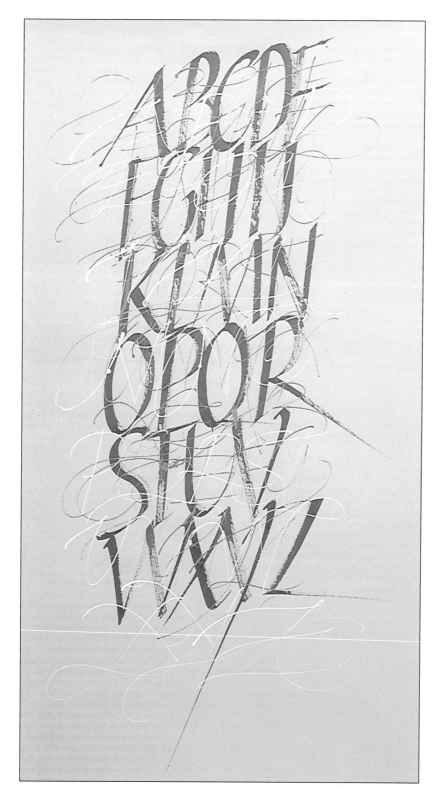

Gaynor Goffe
ALPHABET DESIGN

*69 x 40.5 cm (27 x 16 in)
Ink and gouache on Ingres
paper, using an automatic
pen.*

**David Nicholls
(Oxford)**
SHAKESPEARE
QUOTATION

*15 cm (6 in) diagonal
Gouache on Japanese
paper; iridescence of frame
produced with anyline
dyes.*

WE ARE SUCH
STUFF AS DREAMS
ARE MADE ON
AND OUR LITTLE
LIFE IS ROUNDED
WITH A SLEEP

Cindy Wonnacott
CHAIN MAIL

75 x 40.5cm (29 1/2 x 16in)
Metal nibs on Ingres paper.
Gouache and resist.

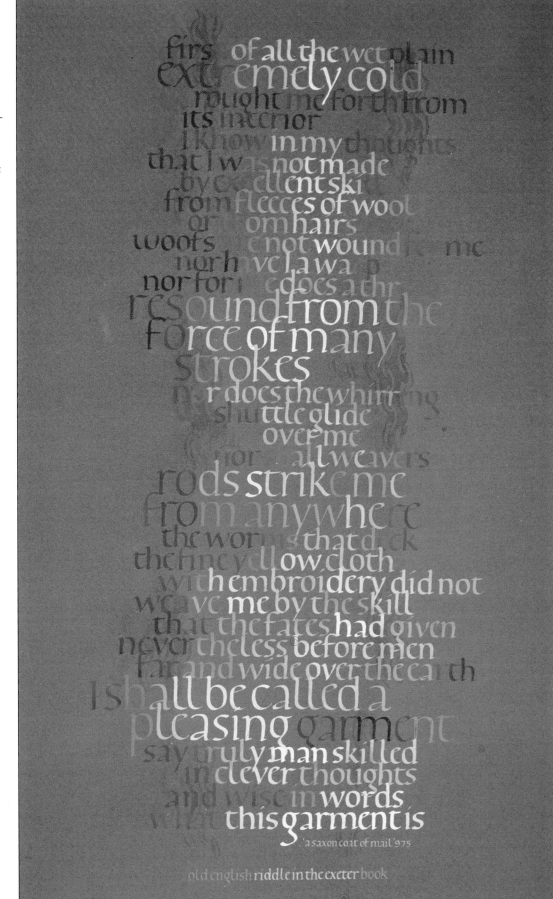

INDEX

ACKNOWLEDGMENTS

*The author would like to thank Bob Kilvert for allowing
publication of his watercolour wash techniques for
the first time. Those interested in exploring these techniques
further can attend one of the courses he runs at
The Old Corner House, Broad Street, Weobley, Hereford HR4 8SA.
The author and publisher would also like to thank the following
people and organizations:*

pp 8-12 The Dean of St Albans Cathedral; **p 17** Bridgeman Art
Library; **pp 24-9** *Everybody's Wine Guide* by Anthony Hogg, Quiller
Press. Maps reproduced by permission of Peter Dominic; **p 33** Pollock
and Searby Ltd; **p 35** Messrs C. Hoare & Co; **p 41** (bottom) *David H.
Nicholls*; **pp 72-6** Reference should be made to Sam Somerville's excel-
lent chapter in *The Calligrapher's Handbook*, 'Parchment and Vellum'.
Expanded from an article published in *The Scribe*, No 44.;
p 77 (top) First illustrated in The Scribe, No 43; **p 85** (bottom) *Chinese
Poems* by Arthur Waley. Unwin Hyman; **pp 106-7** *The Pillow Book of Sei
Shonagon* edited and translated by Ivan Morris (Penguin Classics
1967) © Ivan Morris, 1967 Reproduced by permission of Penguin
Books Ltd; **p 109** (top) *Revelations of Divine Love* by Julian of Norwich,
translated by Clifton Wolters (Penguin Classics, 1966) © Clifton
Wolters, 1966 Reproduced by permission of Penguin Books Ltd; **p 119**
(bottom) Reprinted by permission of Faber and Faber Ltd from
Markings by Dag Hammarskjold translated by W.H. Auden and
Leif Sjoberg.